Raising Godly Children in an Ungodly World

Leaving a Lasting Legacy

EDITED BY TODD A. HILLARD

Ken Ham | Steve Ham

Presented to

_____

From

_____

Date

_____

on the Occasion of

_____

_____

Your Legacy of Faith

First printing: August 2008
Sixth printing: March 2015

ISBN: 978-0-89051-542-6
ISBN: 978-1-61458-072-0 (ebook)
Library of Congress Number: 2008932785

Unless otherwise noted, all Scripture is from the NAS95 Version of the Bible.

Previously published under the title *Genesis of a Legacy*

Photos on pages 90, 150, and back cover by Lee Lynch, Lynch Photography, Union, Kentucky

Cover design by Left Coast Design, Portland, Oregon

Please consider requesting that a copy of this volume be purchased by your local library system.

Printed in the United States of America

Please visit our website for other great titles:
www.masterbooks.net

For information regarding author interviews, please contact the publicity department at (870) 438-5288.

Master Books®
A Division of New Leaf Publishing Group
www.masterbooks.net

This book is dedicated to our living siblings,

Rosemary, Beverley, and David;

and to our brother Robert,

who now lives face to face with his Creator.

May it be a remembrance of the godly heritage our

family was given, and a reminder to all of us to pass on

to the next generation that which was entrusted to us

concerning the Word of God.

The Ham family at Mundoo near Innisfail in North Queensland in 1962 — a ready-made Sunday school to start at Mundoo. Steve was not yet born.

contents

Introduction 9

Prologue: Leaving a Lasting Legacy — *Ken Ham* 13

PART 1: THE FOUNDATION OF A LEGACY 22

   1. Dead Men Do Tell Tales — *Ken Ham* 25

   2. If All We Had Was the Word — *Steve Ham* 41

   3. The Theologian in Each of Us
       — *Ken and Steve Ham* 55

PART 2: THE COMPONENTS OF A LEGACY 70

   4. Godly Generations — *Ken Ham* 73

   5. God Has No Grandchildren — *Steve Ham* 91

   6. Diligent Dads — *Ken Ham* 103

   7. A Girl Named Ruth — *Ken Ham* 115

PART 3: BUILDING A LEGACY 132

   8. Creating the Environment of Sanctification
       — *Steve Ham* 135

   9. Welcome to the War — *Ken Ham* 151

  10. Vegemite Kids — *Ken Ham* 171

  11. Submission, Discipline, and Nutrition
       — *Steve Ham* 189

  12. The Family Fortress — *Steve Ham* 211

Epilogue: The Revelation of a Legacy — *Ken Ham* 229

Ken Ham reading to his grandchildren

introduction

with Ken Ham

This is a very different book — certainly different from anything I've written so far. It is part journal, part tribute, part devotional, and part "how-to." It's also *all heart,* an expression of a passion, conviction, and commitment to the Word of God — all of which was instilled in us by our parents. My brother Steve and I deeply desire that the words ahead will be real and honest as we offer glimpses into our childhood and adult lives. As we share with you our journeys in the Ham family, you will see us, warts and all. We will share stories from when we were being raised in Australia, a country that by anyone's standards would be considered non-Christian and pagan. I'll talk about my years as a student and a teacher, and about the surprising paths that brought me to where I am today as one of the leaders of the worldwide Answers in Genesis ministry. Steve and I pray that the words ahead will bring glory to God for all He has done — and all He continues to do — for my family and yours as well.

In my capacity as a speaker for Answers in Genesis, I write and speak most often on topics related to the creation/evolution debate and Genesis. Over the years I have also developed messages about how the Genesis foundation (and the doctrines that are built upon it) impacts day-to-day life. My brother Steve has done the same, developing Genesis-based talks dealing with raising children.

Steve and I are greatly concerned with the condition of many church families. The statistics are discouraging, and the situation appears to be going from bad to worse, with the possibility that much of the next generation could be entirely lost to the ways of the Lord. Because of our unique upbringing and our understanding of the authority of the Word of God, we have been convicted to write this book in the hope that many more godly offspring will be produced for the Lord; for we believe the trends we see can be reversed, one family at a time.

To that end, this book is about the family — the Christian family. Specifically, we will do our best to answer this question: *What does God's Word teach us regarding roles of parents and how to bring up children?* As we find answers to these overriding questions, other important questions will be answered as well:

- Why is the family disintegrating?
- What is a godly legacy and why is it vital to our families and our society?
- What is God's purpose and meaning for the family?
- What is the primary importance of marriage?
- How do we know God's Word is an all-sufficient parenting guide?
- How do we interpret and apply the Bible to our parenting with integrity?
- Why is our relationship with Christ the most important element of a legacy? What are God's roles for the husband and wife in a family?
- How do you create a family environment for spiritual growth?

- How are we to train our kids and place ourselves in a position to answer our children's potentially faith-shattering questions?
- Is Christian education an option?
- Should all children be home schooled?
- Are Christian children meant to be salt and light in the public schools?
- What does the Bible say about "submission"?
- How are we to implement godly discipline and teach our children discernment?
- What is a "family fortress" and why is it important to the world?

The answers to these vital parenting questions (and many, many more) are found in the Bible, starting with the Book of Genesis. The sufficiency and authority of Scripture, properly interpreted and understood, gives us the basis for godly parenting. As you take God's Word and apply its eternal principles to the everyday issues you face with your family, you will begin to create a godly heritage — a legacy that will impact the generations to come in ways you never dreamed possible.

I am, by God's grace, the head of a major Christian organization, and an author of many books. Through our websites, conferences, radio programs, and written literature, God is using the ministry of Answers in Genesis to influence thousands of lives throughout the world on a daily basis. As we address these vital topics regarding parenting, Steve and I will share, as best we understand them, the influences which have guided our lives and shaped us into who we are today. We also lay down the biblical foundation for raising godly children that we have learned with our wives over many years. As we share with you our family struggles and obvious imperfections, it is our hope that our honest and personal words will communicate our life experiences to you in a way that is serious, at times humorous, and, hopefully, very convicting.

So be prepared to be challenged as we share with you *Raising Godly Children in an Ungodly World!*

Stephen and Trish with Mum and Dad on their wedding day, July 29, 1989.

leaving a lasting legacy

with Ken Ham

A good man leaves an inheritance
to his children's children
(Prov. 13:22).

On the northern tip of Australia lies a nondescript outpost called "Thursday Island." Sparsely inhabited by indigenous people from Papua New Guinea, and surrounded by the deep blues of the sea, the small and quiet community serves as the commercial center for the Torres Strait Islands, a small cluster of tropical islands just off of Cape York.

On the 22nd of October, 1928, a child came into the world on this little-known island; his birth going unnoticed by all except a few. It was an unremarkable entrance into human existence, in an unremarkable location, far from the cities and headlines that concerned the rest of the world at that time.

The second of two children, the child grew through humble means and hard work in a land that was raw and full of potential. As the son of an educator, he learned his lessons well, many of them the hard way. He made music upon the violin and mandolin and learned his three R's by the light of a gas lamp when the day was through.

When he was 16, his father died. With no earthly father to guide him into adulthood, he turned to his Heavenly Father for direction, stability, and a model after which to shape his life. In the words of the Bible he found all he needed; the Book fed both his passion for learning and his heart for his Lord and Creator.

As the world began to heal from the wounds of World War II, the son of the educator chose to become an educator himself, investing his career in the next generation as a teacher, administrator, and principal. With his new bride in one hand and his Bible in the other, he set out to make an eternal difference in his world. As his passion for truth and the lost continued to grow, he became a powerful and articulate defender of his faith and the Word he so desperately loved, in his home, his schools, his church, and his community.

Then, on October 20, 1951, in the northern town of Cairns, he did a most remarkable thing: He became a father — but not just any father; he became *my* father — the man I will forever call "Dad." On the day I was born he became the most important man I would ever know on the face of this earth.

With a family now in tow, and the decades beginning to slip away, he seized every day as an opportunity to influence his world for truth and to shape his children into those who would love God and His Word. Through his words and through his life, he imparted lessons that will be forever etched in my mind and in the hearts of my four living siblings, and in the heart of my late brother Robert:

Whatever you do, you do it 100 percent.

Dad never did anything half-heartedly. If it was worth doing at all, he did it as best he could. His reports as an educator were first class; his interaction with students and other teachers was always focused and intentional. He had chosen to serve the world as an educator, but he approached the task with an intensity that reflected the truth in Colossians 3:23:

> Whatever you do, do your work heartily, as for the Lord rather than for men, knowing that from the Lord you will receive the reward of the inheritance. It is the Lord Christ whom you serve.

In those days, Australian educators were transferred every few years as they climbed the promotional ladder. Approximately every three years or so we would pack up the family and move to a different location throughout the state of Queensland. Finally reaching the top as a principal of a class 1 school, we settled down in the city of Brisbane, where he continued his work and his parenting with passion and devotion.

What you do at the top filters down and brings others up. Dad showed us that a leader has responsibility, because those who follow are greatly influenced by the one out in front. In Luke 6:40, Jesus said:

> A pupil is not above his teacher, but everyone, after he has been fully trained, will be like his teacher.

By his example, Dad illustrated this truth in clear ways, both in his schools and in our home. Who we are impacts those in our charge, either for good or for bad. While other principals (and many teachers) hit the pub after work and wondered why their teachers were sluggish in the mornings, Dad upheld his moral integrity . . . and his teachers and faculty followed. His schools were simply the best in the territory.

Invest where it counts. Through our parents, we learned about godly generosity. Our house was a well-known stopping-off point for missionaries, and Mum and Dad freely gave whatever assistance they could to ministers of the Word — they had such passion to see the gospel proclaimed and people saved. On one occasion, a missionary needed money to continue his journey, and my parents gave him the little they had, never letting on what a phenomenal sacrifice it was for them.

If my parents acquired some household goods, resulting in them not needing a piece of furniture or some other item, they would look for a needy person to give the excess piece. Generous with their finances, possessions, and time, they always exhibited such joy in helping others. They understood and practiced Matthew 6:19–21:

> Do not store up for yourselves treasures on earth, where moth and rust destroy, and where thieves break in and steal. But store up for yourselves treasures in heaven, where neither moth nor rust destroys, and where thieves do not break in or steal; for where your treasure is, there your heart will be also.

As their children, we recognized that the Lord is good and generous, so why not help others? Where did I learn that? Mum and Dad for sure.

Take action and take risk. Dad was a risk taker and a man of action. He and Mum never really wondered how to get something done, they just did it. Whether it was bringing missionaries into town for a campaign, starting a Sunday school, or giving more than they reasonably should, they rarely counted the costs. If they felt the burden that something should happen, they made it happen. They were like Nehemiah, who, when he saw the walls of Jerusalem and the temple of God in ruins, was burdened to do something about it. When he saw the leaders treating the people unjustly, he asked the question "Why isn't someone doing something?" He acted and took it upon himself to rebuild the holy city and ensure justice for the people. Daniel 11:32 says:

> The people who know their God will display strength and take action.

My father and mother were known as people of strength and action, even when the task before them was filled with great risk. Did this affect us as their children? Of course it did. When they took risks and acted, we saw time and time again the provision of God, giving us the faith to act as well. Like my father, I've been a risk taker, too. When I look at the history of Answers in Genesis I just shake my head. I don't know how we did it back then, and I don't know how we are doing it now. The people involved, the growing vision, the incredible provision of God every time we take a step . . . it's miraculous, I think. I doubt I ever would have learned to take risks (which are really just steps of faith, carefully and prayerfully thought through) and to take action had I not grown up with the model of my parents.

Defend the faith wherever you might be. Australia is quite a large country; about the same size as the 48 states of the continental United States. The population, however, is rather small, currently about 19 million. It is a land of rich natural resources, but spiritually, it is a dry, dry desert. The number of born-again Christians in my homeland is probably only two percent. Only five to seven percent attend churches of any kind. In this land of great spiritual need, our parents instilled in us the conviction to be missionaries and defenders of the faith, no matter where we happened to be.

Some of the small towns we were transferred to only had one or two churches, and sometimes there were no Sunday schools at all in the rural areas where Dad's school was located. I remember my parents starting up Sunday schools so they could reach children with the truth of God's Word and the gospel. Sunday after Sunday they would drive from house to house, picking up kids and packing them in the car like sardines . . . with no seatbelts, of course. (I know, you could get arrested for that today, but back then it's just what they did to do what they knew had to be done.)

The lack of churches in the cities we lived in often made it difficult to find one that stood on the authority of God's Word. Not all the churches we attended had pastors who took the stand they should have on God's Word. Many times I recall my father, with my mother and us children in tow, going up to the pastor after a service. With Bible in hand he would challenge the pastor about some of the things he said in his sermon, quoting Scriptures that resounded with the words "Thus said the Lord," or "It is written. . . ." Dad just loved the passages that proclaimed "Thus says the Lord," "It is written," and "Have you not read . . . ?!" (To this day, when I quote verses that contain these phrases, an image of my father confronting liberal pastors pops into my mind!)

As we were transferred around, my father served on many different deacon/elder boards of churches throughout the state of Queensland. Often he would come home from a meeting really upset that someone didn't seem to want to take a stand on issues he believed were vital. Whether it was Sunday school material, mission outreach, or discipline that needed to be applied to a wayward member, my father wanted to do what God's Word clearly taught, but many times others in leadership didn't want to "rock the boat," or they wanted to smooth over the situations without confrontation. Not our dad. He wasn't afraid to shake things up when necessary. I heard them call Dad "Merv the stirrer" because he didn't hesitate to jump in and ruffle some feathers if the integrity of the Word was at stake.

Was he correct in all instances? Of course not, and I'm not even aware of all the situations he was involved in. Even if my father wasn't always right in every situation, I know his heart was in the right place every time. To the best of his understanding, he wanted to do things God's way. If that meant being called a "stirrer," then so be it. He put God's Word before losing church members or friends if someone needed confronting in a biblical manner.

We learned that vital lesson well as his children, and it's important that you do the same. If you take the Bible seriously, live by it, and defend it when it is compromised, you will likely be tarred with the same brush. Both my brother Steve and I have experienced the same stereotyping as my father. No matter how graciously you put across scriptural truth, you will also potentially be viewed in a similar manner.

Yes, Dad was considered a "boat rocker," and he was prepared to make waves when necessary. He felt that if you needed to create a tsunami to make things right, then so be it. Sure, he cared about what people thought of him, he cared about them very much . . . but he cared about the Bible more. The Word of God was the foundation of his life. It was the air in his lungs and the blood in his veins. He never ceased to read it, contemplate it, apply it, and defend it. In 2 Timothy 4:1–5, Paul exhorted Timothy with a great challenge, a challenge that my father accepted as his own:

I solemnly charge you . . . preach the word; be ready in season and out of season; reprove, rebuke, exhort, with great patience and instruction. For the time will come when they will not endure sound doctrine; but wanting to have their ears tickled, they . . . will turn away their ears from the truth, and will turn aside to myths. But you, be sober in all things, endure hardship, do the work of an evangelist, fulfill your ministry.

Daily, he would study and study so he could be prepared to defend the Christian faith against false teaching and the claims that the Bible contained contradictions. Whether it was the worldwide Flood, the feeding of the 5,000, or arguing against the possibility that man evolved from molecules to ape to man over millions of years, Dad defended the Word of God as if his life depended upon it . . . which, in fact, it did.

He was always very adamant about one thing – if you can't trust the Book of Genesis as literal history, then you can't trust the rest of the Bible. After all, every single doctrine of biblical theology is founded in the history of Genesis 1–11. My father had not developed his thinking in this area as much as we have today at Answers in Genesis, but he clearly understood that if Adam wasn't created from dust, and that if he didn't fall into sin as Genesis states, then the gospel message of the New Testament can't be true either.

When it came to apparent contradictions or scientific conflict, he would say something like this: "Kenneth, even though I don't have the answers in this area doesn't mean there aren't any — it just means we don't have them at this time. We need to ask God to provide us with answers — but even if He doesn't, this is no reason to reject God's Word."

Dad, by example and through his teaching, had helped me understand something that has been with me since that time: When something we learn contradicts Scripture, we need to first of all go to the Bible and study the words in context very carefully. If, after doing this, we are sure the Bible still clearly means what we had previously gleaned, then we need to question the ideas that contradict the Bible's words. Then, even if we can't find an explanation that shows where the secular idea is in error, we need to continue to search and wait for the answer. Even if we don't find answers in our lifetime, we cannot reinterpret Scripture. To do so would be to make man's ideas infallible and God's Word fallible. This would put us on a course of compromise and unbelief through the rest of Scripture, and Dad often warned us of this "slippery slope."

****

These were some of the lessons we learned from our parents; lessons that shaped our lives in every way and continue to shape the lives of our children and those around us. God used them both to impact our lives in ways we still cannot imagine. In the end, their example taught us vital priorities: We learned that life was to be lived with God first, others second, and self third.

Throughout my childhood and teenage years, two aspects of Dad's life made impressions on me more than all the others. First, he hated compromise. He would never knowingly compromise the Word of God, and he took the scriptural warnings about compromise, purity of doctrine, and contending for the faith very seriously.[1] Second, he obeyed the pointed command made in 1 Peter 3:13–15:

> Who is there to harm you if you prove zealous for what is good? But even if you should suffer for the sake of righteousness, you are blessed. AND DO NOT FEAR THEIR INTIMIDATION, AND DO NOT BE TROUBLED, but sanctify Christ as Lord in your hearts, *always being ready to make a defense to everyone* who asks you to give an account for the hope that is in you, yet with gentleness and reverence (emphasis added).

Okay, in all honesty, he sometimes forgot about the "gentleness and reverence" part (none of us Hams will ever claim he was perfect!), but he had the rest of the passage down firm. He would stand up strongly for what he believed was true. He was a leader who listened to advice, but he was never intimidated by people who weren't willing to suffer in order to stay true to the Word of God.

He was an uncompromising witness and defender of the gospel. God used him to lay a rock solid foundation for our family and prepare us not only for this present life — but also for an eternity with our Creator. I cannot fathom the value of this inheritance which he left me. There is no doubt in my mind that the legacy of my father and mother, together with the Lord's calling on my life, is the reason I came to be in the ministry of Answers in Genesis — now reaching millions of people around the world.

Who would have guessed that God would use a simple man like my father to shape our family in such powerful ways? Who could have speculated that through the faithful obedience of a boy from Thursday Island and the humble devotion of the woman we still call our Mum, God would choose to make such an impact on the world?

They were simple vessels that served a mighty God. As their children and His, we will be eternally thankful to the One who loaned them to us, who guided them with His Word, and who empowered them with His Spirit to raise a godly family in an ungodly world.

> He who is the blessed and only Sovereign, the King of kings and Lord of lords, who alone possesses immortality and dwells in unapproachable light. . . . To Him be honor and eternal dominion! (1 Tim. 6:15–16).

Endnotes

1. See Ps. 18:30; Ps. 56:4; Ps. 103:20; Ps. 119:1–176; Matt. 12:5, 19:4, 22:31; Mark 12:10; Luke 6:3; Phil. 1:10; 1 Tim. 1:5; 1 Pet. 1:22.

PART 1:

THE FOUNDATION OF A LEGACY

Therefore everyone who hears these words of Mine, and acts on them, may be compared to a wise man, who built his house on the rock. And the rain fell, and the floods came, and the winds blew and slammed against that house; and yet it did not fall, for it had been founded on the rock (Matt. 7:24–25).

Dear Lord Almighty,

May we acknowledge You as the creator and sustainer of all things. May we seek to glorify Your name in all that we do and say. Please give us Your wisdom and power as we seek to act in the stewardship of the precious gifts of our children. Please help us in the delivery of Your Word that they may be truly adopted as Your children. Help us to use Your Word to discern truth from lies in this deceiving world. Please help us to be consistent in our approach to biblical parenting. Please save our children.

We love You, our mighty God. Thank You for the heritage You have given us in our children. Please help us not to let You down but to honor You in all we do.

Amen

Ken and Rosemary with Mum and Dad in 1955 — taken at Mackay, North Queensland, while Dad was teaching at a local school called Sybil Creek.

CHAPTER 1

dead men do tell tales

with Ken Ham

> . . . the righteous shall be in
> everlasting remembrance
> (Ps. 112:6; NKJV).

legacy (lĕg´e-sē) *n.* Something handed down, by one who has gone before in the past, and left to those in the present and future.

There is a saying, one that we have gathered from the legends of the Wild West, which says "Dead men tell no tales." The saying implies that the knowledge and influence of the deceased goes with them to the grave, never to be heard from again. I find that not to be the case! Dead men *do* tell tales. If you ever take a walk around the small English town of Bedford, as I have, you will quickly see what I mean.

Bedford was the hometown of John Bunyan, author of the still very popular *Pilgrim's Progress,* now in its 400th year of printing.[1] The day I walked around the town, I saw reminders of John Bunyan everywhere — the site of the jail where he spent many years imprisoned, the site of the house in which he was raised, his statue in the town square, the church he preached at in later life with a museum of many of his personal items, and the church where he was baptized in 1628. Bedford even has a pub called "Pilgrim's Progress Pub!" (I'm sure John Bunyan would *love* to know he had a pub named after his famous book!)

Something really hit me as I walked around Bedford. As I thought about the life of John Bunyan and how he was persecuted and jailed for preaching the Word of God, I wondered about what happened to those responsible for his persecution and jailing. There was no mention of any of Bunyan's enemies in Bedford. In fact, in the large graveyard of the church where Bunyan rang the church bell as a child, I saw many very old gravestones. It is certainly possible that some of these gravestones stand on the graves of Bunyan's persecutors. However, these gravestones were so eroded that the names had disappeared. Whoever these people were, their memory has all but gone. As I looked at these nameless gravestones, Proverbs 10:7 came to mind:

> The memory of the righteous is blessed, But the name of the wicked will rot.

Certainly, this is the case in Bedford. The man who stood for the authority of the Word of God is remembered. The memory of those who opposed Bunyan has disappeared into oblivion. Bunyan and his books (particularly *Pilgrim's Progress*) live on in the memories of people all over the world and in the printed pages that still come off the printing presses today. Yes, "The righteous shall be in everlasting remembrance."

A very similar type of situation exists in the town of Worms, Germany. My wife, Mally, and I walked around this town, finding many memorials to Martin Luther, the great reformer who started the Reformation in 1517.[2] There were various statues, plaques, and other markers that told the story of Martin Luther. I even had the awesome opportunity to stand at the very place where it is believed Luther stood when he was purported to have uttered these now famous words:

> ### Here I stand [on Scripture]. I can do no other. God help me! Amen.

I must admit, tingles went down my spine as I stood there and contemplated the life of a man who started a movement that has affected the world for the Lord to this day.

Again, I didn't see any memorials to all of those who opposed Luther. They aren't remembered in Worms; the memory of those who persecuted him is all but lost. Luther — the man who stood for the authority of the Word of God — is remembered, and his legacy continues to have great impact on the world today . . . even among those who don't know his name. The righteous *shall* be in everlasting remembrance; but unfortunately, the *unrighteous* can still make an everlasting impact as they forge legacies of an entirely different kind.

If you walk the streets of Shrewsbury, England, you will find memorials to another man of great influence — memorials quite similar to those left for Bunyan and Luther. There is a statue outside his school and a sign outside of the home of his birth, noting the date of February 12, 1809. This is the birthdate of Charles Darwin, who at the age of 50 would publish *On the Origin of Species*. Throughout the town a similar pride is felt and is reflected in the names of many locations: Darwin Gardens, Darwin Terrace, Darwin Street, and Darwin Shopping Center.

There are similarities in the memorials to these three men, but the legacies they left behind could not be more different. Darwin proposed that "life" can be explained without God. By concluding that a supposed link between ape and man meant that there is no God (as detailed in his subsequent book, *The Descent of Man*), his ideas left humanity to decide right or wrong on their own, to write their own rules and do their own thing, following whatever seems best in their own eyes.

The implications of Darwin's legacy are far-reaching. He paved the way for moral relativism, and fueled racism (claiming that blacks, aborigines, and others are inferior, less-evolved races.) His ideas have also fueled the abortion industry, leading to the conclusion that an unborn child is nothing more than a lump of cells (or just an animal) and that a woman has the right to kill it if she so chooses. The ideas of Darwin even paved the way for Hitler, who used them to justify the extermination of those he considered less than ideal — resulting in the mass murder of millions of Jews, gypsies, and others. His ideas have contributed to the erosion of the family, educational institutions, the decay of the legal system, and have led to great compromise in the Church.

To see evolutionary measures and tribal morality being applied rigorously to the affairs of a great modern nation we must turn again to Germany of 1942. We see Hitler devoutly convinced that evolution provides the only real basis for a national policy.[3]

One of the students involved in the Columbine (Colorado) school shootings wore a T-shirt with "natural selection" written on it. The more students are told they are just animals, and have evolved by natural processes — the more they will begin to act consistently with this view of origins. As generations are trained to believe there is no God, thus no absolute authority, then there is no basis for determining right and wrong — moral relativism will pervade the culture.

The late Dr. Carl Sagan and his wife Ann Druyan wrote an article that appeared in *Parade Magazine*, April 22, 1990, using the fraudulent idea of embryonic recapitulation popularized by Ernst Haeckel (the false idea that when an embryo develops in its mother's womb it goes through a fish stage, etc., reflecting its evolutionary history, until it becomes human) to justify abortion. They claimed the embryo wasn't really human until about the sixth month.

I've heard of girls who were told by an abortion clinic that what was in their womb was in the fish stage of evolution, thus they could abort it. A false view of origins leads to terrible consequences.

For example, families are breaking apart due to evolutionary views of unborn children as nothing but animals, and subsequent abortions that result. School shootings such as those at Columbine High School are prevalent among secular schools, because students view other students as animals. The ideas of Darwin are having an effect throughout the culture.

This is the Darwinian legacy: A false idea that has led to the destruction of the authority of the Word of God in our modern age. He popularized a philosophy that has convinced others that the Bible is not true, that everything is the result of random natural process, and that we are little more than animals; free to decide as we are bidden to decide.

Two signs outside of the Shrewsbury Unitarian Church speak for themselves. The first proudly proclaims:

Charles Darwin worshiped here when he was young.

The second church sign, permanently etched as a motto to be seen by all who pass by, gives a clear indication of the legacy behind which the legacy of Darwin emerged:

No one has the only truth, this we believe.

Not a Question of "If"

Luther, Bunyan, and Darwin; these three men left two entirely different kinds of legacy. Each legacy continues to impact the world in different ways. Let there be no doubt: *A legacy is a very, very powerful thing.* Let there be no doubt about this either: *You too will leave a legacy.* Truly, it's not a question of *if* you will leave a legacy, it is only a matter of *what kind.* Long after your body is laid to rest, the impact of your life will continue to spread throughout your community and your world. Never forget that your legacy will be felt most strongly by those closest to you: *your family.*

Your family desperately needs you to stand up and lead, because the world is drawing them in all the wrong directions. Statistics indicate that around 90 percent[4] of the children from church homes attend public schools in America. Sadly, statistics indicate that seven out of ten of such students will walk away from the church after their senior high years.[5]

America is said to have been the greatest Christian nation on earth. This country has the world's greatest number of Christian bookshops, Christian radio stations, churches, seminaries, and Christian and Bible colleges. It is inundated with all of the best Christian resources available, yet America is becoming less Christian every day . . . and many Christian parents are heartbroken to see their children move toward the world and away from the church.

Dads and moms are crying out for answers, and teachers are becoming increasingly concerned by the rebellious attitudes, lack of politeness, and vanishing Christian morals they see, even in "church kids." Barna Research found that only nine percent of teens who call themselves "born-again Christians" believe in absolute moral truth.[6] Family breakups, even among those calling themselves Christian, are startlingly common.[7]

What are the problems? What are the solutions? Are there answers that will deal with the heart of the problems and provide real solutions? Christian and secular books about the family and raising children abound, yet the questions continue. How should children be raised in today's world? How can a family produce godly offspring dedicated to the Lord? What methods of discipline should be used in bringing up children? Should Christian children be kept in public schools to witness to others, or is Christian or home schooling a necessity? How can Christianity be made relevant to the younger generations?

The list of questions goes on and on, and the Christian family of today is deeply struggling to find answers. I believe there are answers — but I want to warn you that they may challenge your comfort zone, and they may go contrary to what is "acceptable" in your community. The answers may be labeled as "offensive" to those who are more worried about political correctness than righteousness.

Before you can even begin to search out and apply the answers, an even more fundamental question must be answered:

What kind of legacy do you intend to leave?
What type of memorials might be
left in your remembrance?

Can I humbly suggest that you can leave a memorial that can affect the world as Luther and Bunyan did? Many of you reading this might be saying, "Give me a break! They were great and now very famous men. They deserve such memorials, but I'll never have statues or other memorials built in my memory. I'm not going to be famous like them."

I disagree with that kind of thinking. You have no idea how God might choose to use you or your children or your children's children. You must understand that God's Word gives us the foundation from which we can do our best to build the right structure in our families. God's Word (not your own wisdom or strength) is the basis of a godly legacy. The Bible alone is living and active, and able to divide and judge correctly, and its principles can lead to astounding results.

If you are going to leave a legacy like Bunyan or Luther, you are going to have to decide to go against the flow, because the flow of the world today is leading to decay, death, and even hell. Each of us has a personal choice to make regarding the future of our family. Will we lead into a legacy of life and freedom based on the Word of God, or will we lead our families into a legacy of relativism and death, as did Darwin?

The question is not rhetorical, but immensely practical, affecting everything that you might do and everything you might be. The type of legacy you choose will most likely have great impact on your community, your world, and, most graphically, your family. Which will it be? Will *you* lead your family into a legacy of truth, life, and freedom based on the Word of God, or will you lead your family into a legacy of relativism, bondage, and death, as did Darwin? It's a decision each one of us must make. I know, I had to do it myself and it was a critical decision in my ongoing journey for truth and answers.

When I started high school, I eagerly looked forward to my science lessons. However, I was perplexed when the teacher taught that humans evolved from "ape-men," and that animals had evolved over millions of years. My textbooks laid out what claimed to be convincing proof that we progressed *from molecules to man* without any outside influence. I was further taught ideas on how the universe had formed — but they all involved naturalistic processes. God wasn't involved at all. They claimed that everything somehow exploded out of nothing all by itself, and they made it all sound so "scientific." Everything I was taught about the origin of matter, life, and man conflicted with what my parents had taught me from the Bible. How was I to resolve this?

I sat down with my father and asked him to help me sort this out. Sadly, at that time there were no books or other resources that we were aware of that dealt with the creation/evolution issue. Certainly, none were readily available to us in Australia at that time. (When I look at all the resources available today, I often think back to this time in my life and realize how blessed people are today.)

From a scientific perspective, my father could not refute the supposed ape-men fossils, or the billions of years of evolution, or the supposed "big-bang" history of the universe. He wasn't a scientist and he didn't understand where these ideas had come from. Although my father had lots of answers in many areas where secular ideas contradicted Scripture, in this area of origins, he just didn't have a defense — he didn't even know where to start.

I completed high school, rejecting molecules-to-man evolution as a philosophy, but I didn't have any solid scientific answers to defend my position. I was concerned about this, but my father's words kept ringing in my ears:

> *Even if we can't find an answer to explain why the secular idea is wrong, we need to continue to search and wait for the answer.*

During my college years while studying for my science degree, I was bombarded with evolutionary ideas in biology, geology, and other subject areas. I still had no scientific response to what I was being taught, so I just lived with the dilemma — though I recognized that sooner or later I had to sort this out in some way. As I studied, however, I did observe that my textbooks and professors did *not* have convincing evidence for Darwinian evolution or the supposed billions of years for the age of the earth. I recognized there were numerous assumptions behind the various interpretations of fossil bones and the supposed long ages attributed to them, but I really wanted some answers.

Somehow, a little booklet that dealt with the creation/evolution issue from a biblical perspective came into my possession. As I read through this booklet, one particular section stood out from all the others. The author stated that from a biblical perspective, there could not have been death and bloodshed of animals and man before sin, since this would destroy the foundations of the gospel. As I thought about this something really hit me between the eyes: *A Christian can't consistently accept the idea of an earth that is billions of years old (with its supposed millions of years of layers of fossils that we know contain evidence of cancer and other diseases in bones), and accept the statements concerning sin and death in the Bible.* Over the years, we have certainly developed such arguments to a much more sophisticated level, but the respect I had for the authority of the Word as instilled in me by my father caused me to recognize the vital importance of this death issue.

This small booklet gave me a number of biblical arguments about why Christians can't accept molecules-to-man evolution and the Bible's record of origins at the same time. For example, Darwinian evolution teaches man evolved from ape-like ancestors, but the Bible teaches Adam was created from dust and Eve was created from his side. Thus, there is no way one can consistently reconcile the Genesis account of the creation of man (if one takes it at face value) with the Darwinian account. These explanations sustained me for some time.

As the years progressed, the Lord confirmed in my thinking that it was important to *wait for answers*, just as my father had trained me. I learned to continue in heartfelt faith, based on what God said in His Word, in spite of a lack of understanding. Passages from Job have helped me considerably in dealing with secular ideas and secular interpretations of evidence when they conflict with what the Word of God says:

> Where were you when I laid the foundation of the earth? Tell *Me*, if you have understanding (Job 38:4).

> Then Job answered the LORD and said: "I know that You can do everything, And that no purpose of Yours can be withheld from You. You asked, 'Who is this who hides counsel without knowledge?' Therefore I have uttered what I did not understand, Things too wonderful for me, which I did not know. Listen, please, and let me speak; You said, 'I will question you, and you shall answer Me.' I have heard of You by the hearing of the ear, But now my eye sees You. Therefore I abhor myself, And repent in dust and ashes" (Job 42:1–6; NKJV).

God aggressively quizzes Job through chapters 38 to 42, asking him questions about various animals and other aspects of the earth and universe that Job cannot possibly answer. "Job, were you there when I made the earth? Do you know this? What about this, Job? Do you understand that? How much do you know about this?" At the end of God's inquisition, Job falls down in dust and ashes, basically saying, "I give up Lord — compared to You I know nothing."

Psalm 147:5 reminds us that "Great is our Lord, and abundant in strength; His understanding is infinite." It is absolutely impossible that we should understand everything . . . yet God *does*, and for the time being, He has given us all the answers we need for a big-picture understanding of life and the universe in His holy and perfect Bible.

My father's words echoed the truth of the Job passages. To this day, I often remember one of the things my father taught me: *If the Bible can't be trusted in one area, how can it be trusted anywhere else?* Dad clearly understood the importance of not compromising God's Word with man's fallible ideas . . . and he taught me to do the same. Looking back on this time, I can't help but think of Proverbs 2:3–6:

Yes, if you cry out for discernment, And lift up your voice for understanding, If you seek her as silver, And search for her as for hidden treasures; Then you will understand the fear of the LORD, And find the knowledge of God. For the LORD gives wisdom; From His mouth come knowledge and understanding (NKJV).

So, as I prayed for answers, I held to my faith in a vacuum of scientific evidence. Still, I felt the conflict between what I thought was "science" and my faith. (I found out later that there is a big difference between "observational science" which we all agree with, and "historical science" which involves the scientist's beliefs about the past.) I really wanted to honor God's Word and find the answers that would validate what I believed to be true. I needed some scientific answers to sort this out; but where would I find them? While I didn't know it at the time, God was working in a special way to provide them for me.

God heard my earnest prayers. In 1974, during my post-graduate year, I mentioned the creation/evolution issue and my dilemma to a friend. He told me about a book that had been published in America which gave lots of scientific answers concerning geology and Noah's flood. Where would I obtain such a book? I traveled into the city of Brisbane to visit the only Christian bookstore I was aware of. It was on the second floor of an old building — not very easy to find. When I described this book on the Flood to the woman looking after the store, she immediately went and found a copy of *The Genesis Flood* by Morris and Whitcomb. (I still have this first major creation book that began my creation library.)

As I read the book, I found so many answers to questions about dating methods, rock layers, fossils, and many other aspects of the creation/evolution issue. I was so excited! They were answers that made sense and clearly showed that observational science *confirmed* the Bible's account of creation and the Flood. (Even though some of the arguments in this book are now out of date, subsequent research built on this publication has only reinforced the overwhelming evidence that confirms the Bible's account of history in Genesis.) My eyes were opened and I began to understand the nature of the scientific arguments concerning the origins issue for the first time. I clearly remember smiling and thinking, *Once again my father's stand on the Scripture has been vindicated — and once again God's infallible Word has judged the pretense of the evolutionists and the compromise of liberal theologians.*

Almost 30 years later, while visiting a particular tourist attraction in Brisbane, an elderly lady recognized me and approached me. As we talked, I realized that she and her husband had owned the Christian bookstore where I purchased *The Genesis Flood*. I explained to her that this was the first major creation book I had obtained, and that it was an integral part of my journey through life. I shared with her that the Lord used that one book to begin a creation ministry in Australia, then Answers in Genesis in the United States, and now many other parts of the world.

She became very excited and told me that her husband had had a real interest in science, the Bible, and the creation/evolution issue. He had such a burden that he made sure he had a copy of *The Genesis Flood* in his bookshop after he found out about it. That book was there on the shelf waiting for me to purchase it.

Soon, I took the book to my father saying, "Dad, I've found many answers to the creation/evolution issue! Observational science *does* confirm the Genesis account!" To this day, I can still picture that smile on his face as he flipped through the pages. He so loved the Word of God and was so thrilled to have adequate answers to uphold God's Word in Genesis. If my father had compromised his stand on the Word before he had the evidence to confirm its authority, I don't believe I would be writing this book or be involved in active ministry today. Thankfully, my father's faith held, and he chose to act on it. In the process, he began a legacy of worldwide influence that neither of us dreamed possible — not from a no-name bunch of outback Australians at least!

****

In a public cemetery in the city of Brisbane, Australia, stands a particular gravestone. The marker is not outstanding in any sense; it is not in any prominent place, nor do tourists gather at this spot. Throughout the city of Brisbane there are neither statues nor memorials in memory of the man whose body rests below the marker.

As one among the thousands of other gravestones, this marker is not easy to find. Unless you were specifically looking for it, there would be no reason to even think about searching for it, or to think it should be noteworthy from all the others, but it is noteworthy to me — even more than those of Luther and Bunyan. The words on this gravestone are few and simple:

In loving memory of HAM, Mervyn Alfred
who passed into the presence of the Lord on 9th June, 1995
Aged 66 years
"For me to live is Christ and to die is gain"
Forever Loved

No signs, no statues, no museum. Our dad, together with our precious and godly mother, will be remembered by memorials of a different kind . . . memorials that will stand into eternity, long after the plaques and portraits of others have fallen. Mum and Dad produced six living memorials in their children, and we, in turn, are now creating a godly inheritance to leave to our children. By the grace of God it will be a godly legacy that will teach and remind people for generations to come about the authority of the Word of God and the saving mercy of our Lord Jesus Christ.

A rag-tag bunch we are, dented and tainted by our own sin. We all have our struggles and battles with the old nature, but we praise the Lord for the godly parents to whom we were entrusted to be trained for our ministries in this world and the next.

Understanding the sovereignty of God, I know I would not be in this ministry if it wasn't for the upbringing my parents gave me. They set the example as dedicated and humble Christians who intentionally sought to raise a godly family that would evangelize the lost in an ungodly world. The Answers in Genesis ministry is itself a memorial to my parents and the legacy they began in our lives and in our world.

Please understand that you too *will* leave a legacy to the generations to follow. They may not build memorials to you and it's unlikely that they will place signs outside of the place of your birth . . . but *what you leave behind will forever impact the hearts and souls of those in your family and beyond. You will leave a legacy; the only question is what kind of legacy will it be.* May you recognize from this day forward one certain thing: The foundation of a legacy worth leaving is made up of a faith in God, and a trust in His Holy Word. All we have to build will either stand or fall on this foundation.

Consider this question: *What will your children say about you when you die?* When your days are done, what kind of legacy will live on in those you touched? Most importantly, will the Lord say *"Well done, good and faithful servant"?* (Matt. 25:21;NKJV).

Key thoughts from this chapter:

1. Everyone leaves a legacy. The only question is *what kind* of legacy it will be.

2. A godly legacy is built on the authority and sufficiency of the Bible.

3. A godly legacy begins with a decision, and may require waiting for answers to certain questions.

4. Leaving a legacy is a big deal. Our children, grandchildren, and the world will be eternally impacted by it.

Questions to consider:

1. Has your community been more influenced by legacies like Bunyan's and Luther's, or have the people around you been more influenced by legacies like the one left by Darwin?

2. What type of legacy did you inherit from your family?

3. Have you ever made a firm decision to leave a godly legacy for your family and your world? If not, please consider doing so now. Your decision *will* make an eternal difference.

Resources and tools:

John C. Whitcomb Jr., and Henry M. Morris, *The Genesis Flood* (Philadelphia, PA: Presbyterian and Reformed Pub. Co., 1961).

Josh McDowell, *A Ready Defense* (Nashville, TN: Thomas Nelson Publishers, 1993).

Greg Bahnsen, *Always Ready* (Nacogdoches, TX: Covenant Media Press, 2004).

Brian Edwards, *Nothing but the Truth* (Darlington, England: Evangelical Press, 2006).

Endnotes

1. *The Pilgrim's Progress* was published in 1678.
2. On October 31, 1517, Martin Luther nailed the 95 Theses to the door of the Castle Church in Wittenberg, Germany.
3. Arthur Keith, *Evolution and Ethics* (New York: G.P. Putnam's Sons, 1947), p. 28.
4. Daniel J. Smithwick, "Teachers, Curriculum, Control: A 'World' of Difference in Public and Private Schools," Nehemiah Institute, Inc., Lexington, KY, 1999, p. 11.
5. T.C. Pinckney, "We Are Losing Our Children," Remarks to Southern Baptists Convention Executive Committee, September 18, 2001.

   George Barna, *Real Teens* (Ventura, CA: Regal Books, 2001), p. 136, states: "If we apply a 'correction factor' to these responses, we would estimate that about one out of three [nearly 30%] teenagers is likely to attend a Christian church after they leave home."

   Barna Research Online, "Teenagers Embrace Religion but Are Not Excited About Christianity," January 10, 2000, www.barna.org/cgi-bin/PagePressRelease.asp?PressReleaseID=45&Reference=D – states: "When asked to estimate the likelihood that they will continue to participate in church life once they are living on their own, levels dip precipitously to only about one of every three teens."
6. Barna Research Online, "The Year's Most Intriguing Findings, from Barna Research Studies," December 12, 2000, www.barna.org/cgibin/PagePressRelease.asp?PressReleaseID=77&Reference=E&Key=moral%20truth.
7. Barna Research Online, "The Year's Most Intriguing Findings, from Barna Research Studies,' December 12, 2000, www.barna.org/cgi-bin/PagePressRelease.asp?PressReleaseID=77&Reference=E&Key=divorce. "Born-again adults are more likely to experience a divorce than are non-born again adults (27% vs. 24%)."

Kenneth Ham, age 8, at Scotsville near Bowen in North Queensland.

CHAPTER 2

if all we had was the word

with Steve Ham

I am holding firm. The biblical
heritage given to me from my
father was really a gift from God, a
special and gracious gift from my
Father above. I am holding firm.

I was born the same year that Ken and Mally met. In
fact, my earliest memories of my eldest brothers and sisters are
of them with their own infant children. Being the youngest
of six children hasn't always been easy. If you have the same
"youngest child syndrome" you will know exactly what I am
talking about. (For those of you who don't, being the youngest
in the tribe is all about doing your best so you'll be recognized
by your siblings as someone other than "just the baby.")

In our family, though, there were also great things about being "just the baby." For starters, my parents had lots of experience by the time they got to me. Ken left home to make his own with Mally when I was barely two years old, and I left home to make my own with Trish when I was 18. My parents were parenting for 38 years with children at home, and we all testify that their foundational parenting platform was a commitment to the Lord Jesus and the belief in every line of His revealed Word.

On top of this, I have also been able to witness the Christian commitment of my parents *and* my elder brothers and sisters. I've experienced a godly legacy being transferred to me as a child and as a sibling. While still a child myself, I watched as my siblings displayed godly parenting in the upbringing of their children — a rare and effective form of mentoring from which I greatly benefited.

Then, after my siblings were off and married, I had the distinct blessing of living as the only child under the roof alone with my mother and father. Looking back, there were times I wish I had had a better attitude and love toward them (I was a teenager in every sense of the word). In spite of me, those years had a great impact on my life as I had the opportunity to simply view every action of my parents without the distractions of having my older brothers and sisters around.

In my memory, I have a very simple yet clear picture of the home I lived in, and three things stand out: my mum, my dad — and a Bible on his lap.

Our father had a relatively simple approach to life, yet it proved to be very powerful and influential:

Dad believed God's Word, and he stood firm on it.

He did not hold the pages of God's Word above God himself, but his deep and uncompromising love for his Savior and Creator gave him a passion for every word of Scripture and the strength to stand and uphold it. The more he read and understood his Bible, the more passion and strength of relationship he had with God . . . and the stronger the relationship became, the more his passion for the Word grew.

I am so thankful that my father took the time (and a lot of it) to study the Bible, and apply its teaching. When I look back at my father's parenting skills, I see another very simple method:

> *Read the Word, believe the Word,*
> *defend the Word; live the Word, teach*
> *the Word — and expose these*
> *things to your children relentlessly.*

So many of us as parents — particularly fathers — are not paying enough serious attention to the study of God's Word. In the short run, it is so much easier to leave careful Bible study to the experts and focus on our own perceived talents. We look for excuses as to why we are not interested in biblical study and biblical family instruction. We look for an easy way out. We look for someone else to do it for us.

Psychology and Substitution

The easy way appears to be for us to turn away from the simple instruction of God's Word, gathered through personal study, and place our trust in a cosmic blend of biblical and psychological ideals and teaching — teachings that more often than not are contrary to the Word of God alone. It is so important that we all realize that there is no substitute for God's Word in any family. The apostle Peter challenges us to "as new born babies, long for the *pure* milk of the word, so that by it you might grow in respect to salvation" (1 Pet. 2:2). No radio or television program, counseling materials, or parenting course can possibly be a substitute for the revelation of our almighty, all-knowing God. Not only that, but the Bible has *all* the instruction we need to raise a godly family. Keep in mind that the Bible was the only resource many of our parents had!

So many of us today think that "parents plus children and a Bible" is a much too simple formula for raising godly children. With all of the parenting courses available these days, parents are led to believe that they have no hope of competent parenting unless they have some strategy given to them by a capable professional. Especially in Christian circles, we spend lots of money and time going to courses in hot pursuit of the right parenting model for our family. I am not saying that doing a parenting course is the wrong thing to do. In fact, there are some good parenting courses providing very practical and helpful tools. The questions remain: What if we had no parenting programs? What if we had no self-help courses? What if we had no trained psychologists? *What if the only parenting book in the household was a Bible?* Would that be sufficient? Could that even be preferred? In Isaiah 28:29 we read:

> This also comes from the LORD of hosts, Who has made His counsel wonderful and His wisdom great.

If God has the greatest wisdom and the most wonderful counsel, who can possibly provide a substitute? Books and courses authored by fallible human beings can *never* take the place of God's Word, nor is there any need for them to do so. The Bible is sufficient and authoritative, and when interpreted properly it gives us all the guidance and information we need to create a godly heritage.

That goes for *this* book as well. My words and Ken's words could never, and should never, be a substitute for His infallible words. However, if this book inspires you to do everything you can to accurately and passionately handle the Word of God, then Ken and I will have passed on some of our heritage to you — the same legacy given to us by our parents. This inheritance has been the foundation of our lives and our families, and it is the one that God has used to grow the ministry of Answers in Genesis, which is built on the truth in relation to the sufficiency of Scripture for *all* we need to know. As Christian parents, the Bible proves its instructional sufficiency to us in many ways. There is no need to look beyond its guidance.

The Function of Scripture

The apostle Paul and Timothy shared a beautiful discipling and mentoring relationship. At the center of this relationship was the Word of God. In 2 Timothy 3:16–17, Paul gives Timothy the reason why Scripture is such a powerful instrument for developing strong Christian convictions and the pursuit of godliness:

All Scripture is God-breathed and is useful for teaching, rebuking, correcting and training in righteousness, so that the man of God may be thoroughly equipped for every good work (NIV).

Let's dissect this vital passage and hear what Paul was communicating to Timothy.

All Scripture Is God-breathed

The Bible is not ours; it's God's. In His awesome power and majesty, God trained a select group of ordinary men and had His Spirit fill their hearts and minds with supernatural inspiration. Through this wondrous sanctifying work, they wrote the very words of Scripture. When it comes to biblical authority, the Westminster Confession of Faith says:

> *The authority of the Holy Scripture, for which it ought to be believed and obeyed, does not depend on the witness of any person or church, but entirely on its author, God (who is truth himself) and therefore it is to be received because it is the Word of God.*

God is the ultimate witness to the sufficiency of His Scripture because God IS.

> *The Word of God is of God — fear it.*

All Scripture Is Useful for Teaching

When Paul says to Timothy that Scripture is "useful for teaching," we must acknowledge the context in which he is using the word "teaching." "Teaching" can mean the actual *process* of communicating and training, or the *content* of what is being taught (the very truth that is within it). In most cases, when we refer to the "teaching of Jesus," we refer to the content rather than the process. In this passage, the Greek word translated "teaching" is *didaskalia*, which relates to the content of the teaching. (The KJV translates it unambiguously as "doctrine.")

This is a significant point, for today in many of our pulpits across the Christian world, God's Word is used within the *process* of teaching, rather than being the very *content* of what is to be taught. Paul is not telling Timothy to use Scripture within the process of his teaching, but to use it because it is completely useful through its content. We must acknowledge the same in our very homes.

The Word of God is God's Word — teach it.

All Scripture Is Useful for Rebuking

Second Timothy 4:2 says:

> Preach the Word; be prepared in season and out of season; correct, rebuke and encourage — with great patience and careful instruction (NIV).

I can remember seeing my father use God's Word in this way many times. While sometimes he may have come across a little harsh in doing so, he never rebuked others with his own words but always used the words of Scripture. Dad was truly "presuppositional" in his approach to the Bible; he saw the world and the words of man through the eyes of the Word of God. He never tried to fit the ways and ideas of man into the Word of God. Used this way, God's Word is the rebuker, not us. This use of Scripture often makes us enemies with the ways and ideas of the world. That's why Answers in Genesis, for instance, has many enemies. That's to be expected. Others may not like it when they are confronted, but we must always be true to His Word.

The Word of God is God's truth — use it to confront lies.

All Scripture Is Useful for Correcting

Paul tells Timothy that the Word of God is useful for "correcting" (2 Tim. 3:16; NIV). We see a great example of this in Acts chapter 2. When the Holy Spirit came upon the believers on the Day of Pentecost, they began to speak in the languages of many of the foreigners in the crowd

(Acts 2:7–8). Some accused them of being drunk, but Peter took a stand and used the Word of God to correct them, quoting from Joel and David. How did the people respond? Acts 2:37 records that "Now when they heard this, *they were pierced to the heart,* and said to Peter and the rest of the apostles, 'Brethren, what shall we do?' Peter said to them, 'Repent, and each of you be baptized in the name of Jesus Christ.' " Peter used God's Word to correct those who were in error, and many were saved that day. God's Word is truly powerful, and a commitment to teaching it is a tremendous asset to those interested in reaching others for the kingdom of heaven, let alone those who desire to raise godly children.

The Word of God is truth — be corrected by it.

All Scripture Is Useful for Training in Righteousness

Not only does the Word of God bring us to justification in Christ through repentance of sin and faith in Him, but the Word also unleashes the sanctifying power of the Holy Spirit so that we might live in His image. That's why Paul tells Timothy that the Word of God is sufficient for "training in righteousness."

In Philippians 3:7–10, Paul exhorts us to realize that compared to "the surpassing value of knowing Christ," all else in life is but "dung" (KJV). Further in this passage Paul shares his desire to "be found in Him (Christ) not having a righteousness of my own derived from the Law, but that which is through faith in Christ." Paul deeply desired to experience and live in Christ's righteousness, even to the point of sharing in His sufferings — even to the point of death — knowing that as a believer, we will receive resurrection to an eternal heavenly prize. How can we stand to gain such a life on earth apart from our commitment to the Lord and His Word to obtain His glorious eternal favor?

As we learn more about God and more about His Word, and as He opens our understanding, we become more like Him in our character. In Romans 12:2, Paul tells us, "Do not be conformed to this world, but be transformed by the renewing of your mind, so that you may prove what the will of God is, that which is good and acceptable and perfect."

Paul is clearly saying that as we apply God's truth to our minds, we will transform *away* from the ways of this world, and walk *toward* the ways of God. This one statement in Romans is really one of the most succinct explanations of sanctification (growing in God's holiness) we will ever come across. To allow more of God's character to permeate and reproduce in our own lives is completely to God's glory.

Sanctification is an understated and underplayed word — not only in the lives of our church members, but also within the environment of the nuclear family. Paul clearly shows us that sanctification happens through the renewal of our minds, and that sanctification is a process in line with God's will. This means it must be a transformation using God's truth, and not our own.

Surely such an important issue should be the desire of every parent. Christian fathers and mothers want to cry out for their whole family to grow in righteousness and intimacy with their maker. If this is our cry, we must acknowledge one very important point: *A very key tool God uses in sanctification is the renewal of our minds to God's good and perfect Truth as revealed in His Word.*

The Word of God is God's holiness — be transformed into His image by it.

. . . that the man of God might be equipped for every good work

With all of the different programs, books, and seminars that call out for the attention of those who desire to serve God, it is no wonder that Paul concludes this passage with a reminder that the Word of God equips "the man of God for *every* good work." That's the answer to the question we asked earlier. Is the Word of God alone sufficient? The answer is a resounding "yes!" If we had nothing else in our church but the Word of God, we would still have everything we would need to be effective as His people. If the Bible were the only blueprint we had to help us build a godly legacy, it alone could equip a parent to do this good work.

The Word of God is entirely sufficient — be equipped by it.

Paul and Timothy — Merv and Steve

Although my father was a strict school headmaster and parent, in the latter years of our relationship we were not unlike Timothy and Paul. In the same way Timothy viewed Paul, I viewed my father as my mentor, teacher, and companion in the Word. In so many ways, the words of my father to me held the same messages as Paul's to Timothy in 2 Timothy 3:14–15:

> But as for you, continue in what you have learned and have become convinced of, because you know those from whom you learned it, and how from infancy you have known the Holy Scriptures, which are able to make you wise for salvation through faith in Christ Jesus (NIV).

Paul gives Timothy a number of charges in chapter 3, and this one reminds Timothy of his biblical heritage and challenges him to be true to it. It is very easy to read over these verses and simply think nice thoughts about Timothy learning "Bible stories" as a child and that Paul is simply telling him to never forget them. It's deeper than that: Paul is charging Timothy to never live down this biblical heritage he has been so wonderfully blessed with by his Lord God. In fact, this passage is also a deep reminder to parents of the responsibility of training children thoroughly in the Word of God!

Timothy lived in Lystra with his mother Eunice, his grandmother Lois, and his Greek father (Acts 16). His mother and grandmother were among the first Christian converts, and they carefully taught him from the Holy Scriptures (2 Tim. 1:5, 3:15). Timothy's mother was Jewish, and I can clearly imagine she and his grandmother sitting down with him and explaining carefully and thoroughly the Old Testament Scriptures about the history of the world, the Law, the prophets, and the coming of the Messiah, Jesus Christ. Through the care of these two devoted women, Timothy learned the very wonders of God, the devastating plight of man, and the redemption that is obtained only through Jesus. That's the kind of teaching that makes you "wise for salvation through faith in Christ Jesus," and that's the kind of teaching our children need, too.

Unfortunately, today we are so distracted from straight biblical teaching. We have been guided away from simple parent/child discipleship, and we have not created a biblically based environment for sanctification in our households. We have replaced these with a focus on behavior modification that attempts to make our homes an easy place to live. Should a parent be more focused on psychology-based behavior modification or biblically based, parental, pastoral care? The answer is obvious.

One of my favorite authors in the world today is John MacArthur. His material is simple and straightforward, and I love his uncompromising stance on the authority of Scripture. In the book *Our Sufficiency in Christ,* he writes the following:

> "Christian psychology" as the term is used today is an oxymoron. The word "psychology" no longer speaks of studying the soul; instead it describes a diverse menagerie of therapies and theories that are fundamentally humanistic. The presuppositions and most of the doctrine of psychology cannot be successfully integrated with Christian truth. Moreover, the infusion of psychology into the teaching of the church has blurred the line between behavior modification and sanctification. . . . If one is a truly Christian psychologist, he must be doing soul work in the realm of the deep things of the Word and spirit — not fooling around in the shallows of behavior modification. . . . There may be no more serious threat to the life of the church today than the stampede to embrace the doctrines of secular psychology. They are a mass of human ideas that Satan has placed in the church as if they were powerful, life-changing truths from God. Most psychologists epitomize neo-Gnosticism, claiming to have secret knowledge for solving people's real problems. There are even those psychologists who claim to perform a therapeutic technique they call "Christian counseling" but in reality are using secular theory to treat spiritual problems with biblical references tacked on.[1]

Based on his studies in the Word of God, MacArthur is convinced that we need to deal with the devastation of sin in our lives before

God, and not come up with humanistic theories simply to deal with the symptoms of sin. We need to understand that our children are born into the natural influence of sin. Psychological behavior modification brings no relief to this problem in humanity. Our only hope is found in the pure biblical principles related to Christ and the Cross, as revealed in God's Word.

As Christian parents, we can all have confidence that the Bible equips us *completely* for being mums and dads. The Word definitely gives parents great wisdom for dealing with a child's behavior. When God's Word is our primary resource, our priority becomes deeply focused on sanctification, rather than wading in the shallows of behavior modification.

God's Word needs to be our primary parenting manual . . . and if for some reason we were to find ourselves with no other guide, His Word would again prove itself to be entirely sufficient. You too can rightly adopt my father's simple approach to life and parenting. God's Word *is* sufficient for all. There is no substitute for its timeless wisdom and authority. If all we had was the Word, that would be enough. In fact, it would be *more*

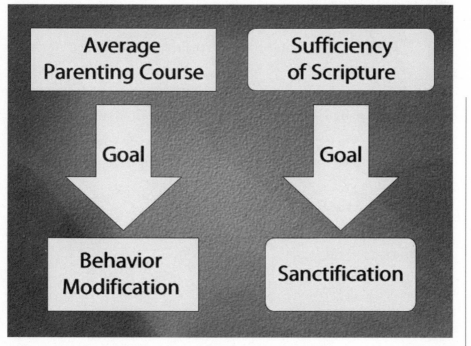

than enough, and its insight alone would leave us better off as we face the challenge of leaving a godly legacy.

I am holding firm. The biblical heritage given to me from my father was really a gift from God. A special and gracious gift from my Father above. I am holding firm.

Key thoughts from this chapter:

1. God's Word is useful for teaching, rebuking, correction, and training in righteousness because it is *of* God and *from* God.

2. While other resources (such as parenting courses or psychological techniques) can be helpful, they can also be harmful and distract us from the pure Word of God.

3. God's inspired Scripture is perfect and absolutely sufficient for equipping us to do the work of God . . . particularly the grand task of raising godly kids.

Questions to consider:

1. Why do you think that people are naturally drawn to worldly philosophies regarding behavior management rather than to the pure instruction of God's Word?

2. In what ways do you see godly and godless principles for raising children being used in your church and your community?

3. What specific steps could you take today to begin using the Word as your primary tool and resource for teaching your children?

Resources and tools:

John MacArthur, *Our Sufficiency in Christ* (Wheaton, IL: Crossway Books, 1998).

Endnotes

1. John F. MacArthur, *Our Sufficiency in Christ* (Wheaton, IL: Crossway Books, 1998).

Celebrating Rosemary's third birthday — 1957 — at Scotsville.

CHAPTER 3

the theologian in each of us

Steve Ham, with Ken

axiom (ak′sē-em) *n.* A self-evident or universally recognized truth.

Do your best to present yourself to God as one approved, a workman who does not need to be ashamed and who correctly handles the word of truth (2 Tim. 2:15; NIV).

Both Ken and I have desired to build this book on two main concepts:

1. Through the gift of God's revealed Word, Christian parents are sufficiently and fully equipped for raising children in an environment built for sanctification. If we had no other resource, God's Word would be more than enough.

2. A forthright defense of the full and sole authority of Scripture is a crucial parental foundation against the world's attempt to keep our children from knowing and growing in God. Authoritative truth has a direct impact on love, purity, conscience, and faith.

Our parents held to these principles tightly. They never explained their model for parenting, but because they lived it consistently, Ken and I have been able to identify it and describe it to you with accuracy. It is interesting to note that neither Dad nor Mum ever completed any formal theological training. In fact, my father was never intimidated or impressed by formal qualifications, even though he graduated from a university to be a teacher. Nonetheless, he always respected his pastors . . . even those he disagreed with.

Dad may not have had a theological qualification, but he was definitely a theologian. Even more than this, he understood every Christian to be a theologian. "Theology" is simply the study of God and the beliefs we hold about Him. Dad understood the study of God to be an obligation of every believer. As soon as he understood someone to hold a position on God or His Word, it resulted in a theological conversation, and he was always excited to engage in it.

If you believe that God sent His only Son into this world to die for our sins, then you have already taken a theological position and you are a theologian, too! Regardless of whether you feel like you are a theologian or not, you are. The point I am trying to make is that everyone needs to take theology and the study of God's Word very seriously.

Please listen to this next statement very carefully: *If the authority of God's Word plays a foundational role in parenthood, then a correct handling, understanding, and consistent application of God's Word is essential to building a godly legacy.* We can't just *agree* that the Bible is foundational; we must *act* on that belief by diligently striving to understand, interpret, and apply the Word in our personal lives and in our homes. We must see ourselves as theologians and endeavor to fulfill that role. Before proceeding, however, it is important to note that biblical theology is a huge subject, and many highly educated men have written volumes relating to it. The study of the things of God is absolutely endless, just as He is. Thankfully, we will have eternity to master the subject! For now, however, we must only move on from where we are and what we already understand.

My father held a very high view of Scripture. As a Christian (and thus a theologian), he had some simple rules that helped him take God's Word seriously. It is my privilege to share two major biblical theological concepts that governed my father's pursuits: 1) What it means to have the Bible as your axiom, and 2) What it means to read the Bible in an "exegetical" manner.

The Bible as Axiom

Dad started with the belief that God's Word is our full and sole authority in *every* matter it deals with — including relationships, history, science, etc. Even before having access to the materials through Answers in Genesis, God used my father's biblical foundation like armor to deflect the humanistic, evolutionary thinking threatening to infiltrate our home.

When you think about it, to be logically consistent, if we accept the claim of the Bible for itself that it is a revelation from the infinite Creator God, then this Word must be the absolute and sole authority to enable us to build our world view (the way we think about everything). The acceptance of biblical authority as *absolute* is paramount to ensuring a consistent starting point. It is totally inconsistent to insist on a biblical foundation, but at the same time accept man's fallible views about the universe and life or somehow try to mix them together.

That's what it means to have "the Bible as axiom." The root of the word "axiom" is the same used for the word "axle." Just as the axle is the central point around which things rotate, the Bible, as our axiom, is to be the central starting point around which all of our beliefs and convictions must revolve. Dad recognized that the Bible was the sole authority in *all* matters of life and practice and in *every* area it touched upon (geology, astronomy, anthropology, child raising, etc.). The Bible was the "axiom" of Dad's life, the central point of truth around which *everything* else revolved.

Recently I was privileged to be a part of a Bible college mission that came to our church. The team conducted a series of evening meetings where friends were invited to hear answers to "why" questions. One of the questions was: *Why is there death and suffering?* I was greatly encouraged as I listened to the principal of the college approach this difficult question. He said that when he reads the Bible, he sees two main parts: Genesis 1–3, and the rest. He explained that the first three chapters in Genesis give us our world view and he showed from the text that when we see things going wrong — such as people dying and suffering — we are constantly reminded that we no longer live in a perfect world, but are part of a fallen and sinful world laced with death.

It was clear from the way that the principal formulated his answer that Scripture was his "axiom of truth." He started with the belief (like a "presupposition") that the first three chapters of Genesis are historically accurate. By building his thinking on the history recorded in these chapters, he was able to put on "biblical glasses," interpreting everything he saw from a biblical perspective (the "glasses" being the history he used to interpret the evidence of the present). His basic understanding was this: Because Genesis is true, we know *sin* has caused all of this death and suffering, and we shouldn't be surprised to see and experience it.

Please recognize at this point that theology isn't a *theory*. Theology reflects *truths* that have great practical importance in day-to-day living. The reality of death and suffering is a prime example. Our family is no stranger to these harsh realities. We understand this as well as any, finding that we have the capacity to sin even as we experience the consequences of living in a fallen and sinful world that is full of suffering and death.

When Ken was a child, he had chicken pox like you have never seen before. You couldn't put a pin between the blisters and the scabs that covered his body. Later, he lived for months with his legs in plaster casts, his tendons having been pulled away from the bones because he was growing too fast. As a teen and an adult, he had a severe case of acne that covered his back and arms (at one point it required a three-month hospitalization, as huge infected cysts blanketed his back, arms, and head).

One of my other brothers, Robert — because of his foundational acceptance of Genesis — described pain, death, and suffering in this world as being *normal;* a natural consequence of the corruption and devastation resulting from original sin. He accepted it and expected it. He even taught about it in a sermon not long before he was diagnosed with a terminal degenerative brain disease at the age of 43.[1]

The issues of suffering and death are just one example of why it is vital that we have a biblical world view. If we use the Word as our axiom, it allows us to rightly interpret what is happening around us. We live in a fallen world, full of death and suffering as a result of sin. As believers, we are not immune, and should not be surprised when these things befall us. Faith doesn't insulate us from the harsher realities . . . the Bible tells us so.

That's what it means to have the Bible as your axiom; you strive to see the Bible as the central starting point for all belief in all matters of life.

Exegesis and Eisegesis

In order to have the Bible as your axiom, it is important to understand that there are two fundamentally distinct ways to interpret and approach your Bible: *exegesis* and *eisegesis*. In simplistic terms, *exegesis* (meaning "out of") is the process of bringing forth the truth *from* the words of Scripture. This entails reading and understanding the context of the passage, who it was written to, and what it was saying to them according to the type of language and literature used at the time. Exegesis takes the Bible "naturally" in a straightforward reading. This is also called the "grammatical, historical, interpretive method" that brings us to practical application.

Eisegesis (i-sa-ge-sis) involves "reading into" a passage by taking God's Word and interpreting it based on human experience, values, and so on. Eisegesis uses *extra*-biblical data to interpret the meaning of the words of Scripture. This approach to Bible interpretation allows us (sinful, fallible human beings) to make Scripture say what *we* believe, and not necessarily

Worldly contradiction is obviously wrong	Worldly contradiction compromises truth of Scripture
The Bible is the full and only authority	Human input for understanding
EXEGESIS	EISEGESIS

what it actually says. Eisegesis starts with human experience and thought and tries to conform the Word to fit in our preconceived ideas. In actuality, *we* then become the authority, not God.

A great illustration of this is found in Ken's talk *Six Days and the Eisegesis Problem*.[2] This talk presents the difference between an exegetical and eisegetical treatment of the text of Genesis 1 as it relates to the six days of creation. Ken walks through the days of creation as they relate to the historical context of Genesis and the Bible as a whole. He also discusses the Hebrew word for "day" *(yom)*, and presents the case that an exegetical study of God's Word allows only one interpretation for the days of creation in the context of Genesis 1 — six literal (approximately 24 hour) days. He then clearly shows that the main reason so many Christian leaders and others in the church don't accept the six literal days of creation is because they are trying to fit the result of some of man's fallible dating methods (which claim the earth is millions of years old) *into* the text (eisegesis), rather than interpreting the dating data according to what is plainly stated in the Word.

This sort of eisegetical treatment allows us to interpret any reference to science or literal history in the Bible as being simply allegorical, metaphorical, or symbolic, but not actual. So often we are told by the world — and even by many teachers in some Bible colleges, seminaries, and Christian schools — that the Bible is a *spiritual* book about man's relationship with God and each other. The Bible is only presented as a book of religion, and we are often told that thinking in areas of science and history should be left to the scholars in those fields.

This is even done when the literal history of the passage and its scientific statements are foundational to doctrine and theology. For example, some Christian leaders claim Genesis 1–11 is meant to be interpreted as an allegory or myth — and yet this section of Scripture is foundational to all biblical doctrines such as marriage and the gospel. If the history and the science of those passages aren't true, then biblical doctrines have no foundation in literal history, and thus can be reinterpreted in any way a person wants.

One of the best theological books I've read is *According to Plan,* by Dr. Graeme Goldsworthy, a former professor of Old Testament, biblical theology, and hermeneutics at Moore Theological College in Sydney, Australia. Dr. Goldsworthy is a sincere man of God. I have read many of his books and respect him greatly. I am using Dr. Goldsworthy as an example because, while he is highly respected and is a strong teacher of biblical principles, his own writings about exegesis show how easy it is to allow man's fallible thinking to invade and distort biblical truth — thus falling into the trap of eisegesis.

In his book, Dr. Goldsworthy takes carefully structured steps to explain the process of exegesis that results in correct biblical theology. In his outline of biblical history from the first chapter of Genesis, he states the following:

> Two comments, however, can be made. First, the passage is unique and thus presents some difficulties in interpretation. The possibilities are far more numerous than a simple choice between strictly literalistic history (usually taken to mean creation in six

periods of twenty-four hours) and non-historical myth (usually taken to mean no relation to historical fact). It is clear that the New Testament texts quoted above (John 1:3, Heb. 11:3; 2 Pet. 3:5–7) understand the creation as an historical event.

Second, when we face such ambiguities, that is, when more than one possible way exists of understanding something in the Bible, the gospel must instruct us since it is God's final and fullest word to man. It is clear from the gospel that God created all things for a purpose, and that He exercises His rule over creation by His Word. It is not at all clear from the gospel that the creation took place in six twenty-four hour periods. Nor is it clear from the gospel that it did not happen in that way. The question is not whether the Bible tells the truth, but how it tells it.[3]

In a previous passage, Dr. Goldsworthy states that he is not entering the six day discussion further than these comments because "it touches on the creation evolution debate." That's unfortunate! Dr. Goldsworthy, while a brilliant, credible, and respected theologian, has in fact used both exegesis and eisegesis to interpret Genesis 1. Through exegetical interpretation, he has clearly shown that the gospel endorses historical credibility to Genesis 1, but because of the "ambiguities" he also suggests that the gospel does not endorse a literal interpretation.

The fact is that the ambiguities that Dr. Goldsworthy is speaking of have only arisen due to man's non-biblical, humanistic (and therefore fallible) interpretation of evidence — particularly in regard to the age issue (millions of years versus thousands of years). The ambiguities are there only because of the influence of evolutionary/millions of years ideas — not because of what the text is clearly saying.

This doesn't stop me from reading Dr. Goldsworthy's books, but it does point out to me how careful Christians need to be in discerning truth, even when it is put to us from great and respected scholars.

We must remember that compromise on one point — even one that might not seem overly significant — can lead to compromise on many others. For example, the secular world view claims that man cannot live for 900 years, but the biblical account in Genesis emphatically states as a matter of history that Methuselah's age was of that order. The secular world view claims that a human virgin cannot give birth to a baby, but the biblical account states clearly that Mary, as a virgin, gave birth to Jesus. The secular world view claims that no man can rise from the dead, but the words of Scripture record as a matter of history that Jesus did rise from the dead — and even point out that if that was not the case, our faith is in vain!

"Moreover, brethren, I declare to you the gospel which I preached to you, which also you received and in which you stand, by which also you are saved, if you hold fast that word which I preached to you — unless you believed in vain" (1 Cor. 15:1–2; NKJV).

"Now if Christ is preached that He has been raised from the dead, how do some among you say that there is no resurrection of the dead? But if there is no resurrection of the dead, then Christ is not risen. And if Christ is not risen, then our preaching is empty and your faith is also empty. Yes, and we are found false witnesses of God, because we have testified of God that He raised up Christ, whom He did not raise up — if in fact the dead do not rise. For if the dead do not rise, then Christ is not risen. And if Christ is not risen, your faith is futile; you are still in your sins!" (1 Cor. 15:12–17; NKJV).

"And God both raised up the Lord and will also raise us up by His power" (1 Cor. 6:14; NKJV).

> *Allowing fallible secular ideas to interpret Genesis 1 opens the door for this to happen with every other passage in the Bible.*

If God's Word alone is not good enough to be taken as written in Genesis 1 (where it is obviously written as history) then why is it good enough to be taken as written in Matthew, Mark, Luke, or John?

The eisegesis problem has wider ramifications, as it eventually makes the Bible and the Church irrelevant. Last year our men's group at church went to a teaching convention in the mountains south of the city of Brisbane. During a question time, the main speaker was asked, "Why are

Australians not interested in coming into our churches anymore; and why are we so apathetic toward spiritual issues?"

The speaker really didn't have an answer, but my brother David, squirming like a worm in his seat, shot to the floor with this follow-up question: "Do you think it is because the Church no longer takes a literal stance in Genesis 1, and therefore presents the world with no answers to their questions?"

I was internally applauding him. The world is asking questions in relation to origins and science and the contradictions between evolutionary ideas and the biblical text. It is obvious that most of the Church really isn't answering these questions. Can you imagine how deflated I felt when the speaker (whom I greatly respect) replied, "We have to take Genesis seriously but not literally." This was an eisegetical statement. What he was really saying was, "Despite the fact that it is obvious that Genesis is history (which is confirmed by the rest of the Bible), I am not prepared to dispute man's fallible interpretation of physical evidence concerning the past. I can't take Genesis literally, but we must take it seriously as there is a message there for us — but we can't tell the world that the message comes from a history we can trust."

The sobering fact is that even among the best of our modern *exegetical* biblical teachers, many are prepared to be *eisegetical* where it suits them — particularly when it comes to Genesis.

Now, you may be asking: How does all this impact our parenting and our commitment to building a godly heritage for our family? *If one can take man's fallible ideas about the origin of the universe and reinterpret Scripture accordingly, then why shouldn't someone take man's ideas about raising children and interpret relevant Bible passages to fit with these humanistic ideas as well?*

How can you show your children you are consistent in your stand upon Scripture? As parents, we have to be well equipped to deal with these potentially faith-shattering inconsistencies we see in our leaders — and help our children to understand why they are being inconsistent.

Your view of the Bible as an absolute foundation for your thinking in every area will determine how you read and teach the Bible to your family. What theological perspectives are you handing on to your children? Are you teaching your children to read the Bible and interpret it correctly — *exegetically*? Are you teaching your children how to read the Bible *consistently*?

The truth is that even though we don't all want to be theologians, we are — and we need to be good ones! Our theological perspectives are being handed down to our children. What an opportunity and enormous responsibility we have to get it right. After all, how we train them will determine how they train their children. Remember what I've said about our dad — and now look at our stand on Scripture! I think our dad's way of thinking has influenced us! How is *your* way of thinking influencing *your* children?!

The Big Picture

with Ken

Because of our father's stand on the authority of the Word of God, the more we studied the Bible and science, the more Steve and I understood that the Scriptures are a revelation from One who knows everything. Because of that, the Scriptures must be foundational to all of our thinking in every area, the axiom of all our beliefs. In most situations, however, we have the choice to either follow in the legacy of Darwin or the legacy of Luther, who stood on the Word of God alone. Whenever the two are mixed, the fallible and the infallible, truth is polluted with error, and they both become fallible.

God's Word is not an exhaustive text book of astronomy, biology, geology, etc., but it does give us a record of the origin of all the basic entities of life and the universe — it's *"the big picture"* of history. We have been given the major events of history in every area to enable us to have the key information to build the right way of thinking about everything. God's Word enables us to have the right foundational information to build the correct way of thinking to understand this present world. It enables us to develop what I call the "big picture" understanding of reality.

As we use this revealed knowledge concerning the past to understand the present, we can use observational and repeatable science to understand more about how this present world operates — and what we do observe should not and does not contradict our way of thinking built upon the Bible.

For example, Scripture reveals that there was a global flood and that death and disease entered the world after Adam sinned. This enables us to have a "big picture" understanding of geology. So when we look at fossil layers like those in the Grand Canyon, we know they couldn't have been laid down before sin because they contain millions of fossils of dead creatures. Because of what the Bible says, we can consider the possibility that Noah's flood may have been the mechanism to lay down the layers. We can then use observational/repeatable science to test the geology, chemistry, etc., to see if the evidence is properly interpreted based upon the revelation of Scripture or the belief in millions of years. Creation scientists have written many books and papers showing that observational science does confirm the biblical "big picture" understanding built from the origins account in Genesis.[4]

When it came to training and raising children, my father had a biblical world view that he applied in his teaching career. He had particular stands on discipline, work ethics, and morality. To the best of his ability and understanding, he had taken the principles laid down in Scripture (because he implicitly trusted this Book to be the infallible, inerrant Word of God) and built a "big picture" understanding to develop a world view he applied to his career in education.

Over time, I came to understand that if the Bible is really what it claims to be, then Christians must do this in *every* area — whether it be morality, science, history, art, music, child raising, etc. The Bible must be the axiom upon which we build all of our thinking. We must stand on the Word of God alone, for our choices can have great implications, not just for us and our families, but for all around us, many of whom have been abused in the legacy of Darwin.

One of the first times this really hit me was during my first year as a science teacher in 1975. In my class were true native Aborigines, tribal descendents of the first tribes that settled in Australia long before the Europeans came. Because of evolutionary thinking, the Aborigines have been oppressed and even killed. Those who committed the atrocities often claimed that the Aborigines (who tend to be shorter and darker skinned than Europeans) were "lower" on the evolutionary chain, and therefore sub-human.

As I taught the class, I made sure that my students were taught the problems with molecules-to-man evolution and the idea that the earth is millions of years old. I shared with them some of the scientific arguments I had gleaned from *The Genesis Flood* and other sources that supported the biblical account of origins. I explained that I did not believe man evolved from ape-like ancestors, but that the account of the creation of Adam and Eve was true — we were all descendants of two people.

I also gave details on the fact that all humans basically have the same skin "color" due to a pigment called *melanin*. I also discussed some of the Australian Aboriginal legends that sounded much like the creation/Flood accounts in Genesis. This enabled me to explain that the Australian Aborigines were descendants of Noah — just like everyone else in the world today — and that the stories they now have were handed down from Noah's time. I continued to show how many years after the Flood, at the Tower of Babel, as a result of the different languages God gave, the human population (and thus the gene pool) split up into different groups and moved out over the earth. The Aborigines must be descendants of one of those groups that moved away from the Tower of Babel.

By my having taught that all humans were of one race and that all are descendents from Adam and Eve, the Aboriginal students were immensely interested and showed great hope and new confidence. The Bible gave them a real place in history and placed them on an equal status with every other human being — including their fellow classmates. The biblical "big picture" had tremendous implications for those who had been victims of Darwinian-based racism.

This incident had a great impact on my own life as well. I became very interested in the topic of the origin of so called "races." At that time I didn't have a lot of understanding about genetics and how the different groups of people obtained certain distinguishing characteristics. This event stimulated me to study this area much, much more. Eventually, I helped write the book *One Blood: The Biblical Answer to Racism*. I also developed talks to challenge the world and the church concerning racism and prejudice.

What happened back in 1975 was part of the training the Lord was taking me through as I developed a Christian world view in every area. This is why Steve and I have attempted to develop what we trust is a truly Christian way of thinking about training children; for when the Bible is the axiom of the home, and the parents strive to be good theologians, the implications are great.

Key thoughts from this chapter:

1. Everyone is a "theologian."

2. The inerrant Word of God must be the "axiom" of all belief, acting as the full and sole authority in every matter.

3. In order to have the Bible as our true axiom, we must interpret Scripture with *exegesis*, where the truth of the Word of God is the obvious starting point. Interpreting the Bible through *eisegesis* makes fallible man the final authority and leads to error.

4. Approaching the Bible as our axiom and interpreting it through exegesis gives us a "big picture" of reality that brings truth into all areas of life.

Questions to consider:

1. If someone looked at your life, would they say you live with the Bible as your axiom? Why or why not?

2. Would you say your current method of Bible interpretation is more exegetical or more eisegetical?

3. What steps could you take to be better at exegesis?

4. What is one issue you are facing where seeing the "big picture" of scriptural truth might bring clarity and decisiveness?

Resources and tools:

Ken Ham, Don Batten, and Carl Wieland, *One Blood: The Biblical Answer to Racism* (Green Forest, AR: Master Books, 1999).

Ken Ham and Carl Wieland, *Walking Through Shadows* (Green Forest, AR: Master Books, 2002).

Endnotes

1. For further information see Ken Ham and Carl Wieland, *Walking through Shadows* (Green Forest, AR: Master Books, 2002).

2. Ken Ham, *Six Days and the Eisegesis Problem* (Petersburg, KY: Answers in Genesis, 2005).

3. Graeme Goldsworthy, *According to Plan: The Unfolding Revelation of God in the Bible* (Downers Grove, IL: InterVarsity Press, 2002).

4. Steven A. Austin, editor, *Grand Canyon, Monument to Catastrophe* (Santee, CA: Institute for Creation Research, 1994).

   Werner Gitt, *In the Beginning Was Information* (Green Forest, AR: Master Books, 2005).

   D. Russell Humphreys, *Starlight and Time* (Green Forest, AR: Master Books, 1994).

   Michael J. Oard, *An Ice Age Caused by the Genesis Flood* (Santee, CA: Institute for Creation Research, 1990).

   Jonathan Sarfati, *Refuting Evolution* (Green Forest, AR: Master Books, 1999).

   Jonathan Sarfati with Mike Matthews, *Refuting Evolution 2* (Green Forest, AR: Master Books, 2002).

   Larry Vardiman, *Climates Before and After the Genesis Flood* (Santee, CA: Institute for Creation Research, 2001).

   John Woodmorappe, *Studies in Flood Geology* (Santee, CA: Institute for Creation Research, 1999).

   Creation Research Society Quarterly – peer reviewed journal published by the Creation Research Society, St. Joseph, MO.

PART 2:

THE COMPONENTS
OF A LEGACY

Train up a child in the way he should go,
And when he is old,
he will not depart from it
(Prov. 22:6; NKJV).

Our Creator and our Father,

We stand humbly before You with a great and grand task before us: the training of our children to be ones that love You and serve You. As we investigate the essential components of that task, and consider our roles and responsibilities in them, we ask that You would reveal yourself to us in fresh and clear ways through Your Spirit and Your Word.

Amen

The growing legacy — the Ham family at "Gumview" at Greenbank in 1989 — Les and Bev's property. Families from left to right: Les and Bev, Robert and Brenda, David and Thelly, Steve and Trish, Rosemary and Paul, Ken and Mally, with Mum and Dad in front.

godly generations

with Ken Ham

When I was growing up, a group of people intentionally removed themselves from the modern world and disappeared into the jungles of the Northern Tropics of Australia. Seeking a liberated and simple existence, free from the pressures and constraints of the world, they left behind their past identity and heritage, shedding their inhibitions (and most of their clothes!). They were known as the "hippies," and their offspring were not familiar with modern medicines or technology. They had little or no respect for society's laws, and many of their children received no formal education. Concepts like "god" and "truth" were not considered important enough to teach. Consequentially, and tragically, they basically degenerated into a non-God-fearing and a non-technological culture in one generation. In less than two decades, they produced a new generation, by and large ignorant of their former heritage and culture — in a sense, we could say it was a "primitive culture."

The lesson is clear: If we don't transmit our knowledge of God to the next generation, it will be lost. Those that follow may not have any means of regaining it, and they probably won't even be aware of the need to do so. This has happened in the past to the New Guinea natives, the American Indians, the North Africans, and many others. All are descendents of Adam, yet somewhere in their past, fathers did not pass on the knowledge they had regarding God and their origins. Thus, when discovered by the Europeans, they were regarded as "primitive."

When the Europeans first discovered the Australian Aborigines, they too were an anti-God spiritist culture. Do you realize that in reality it could have taken only one generation to produce such a culture? Like us, the Australian Aborigines had an ancestor who knew all about the true God . . . and he could even build ships! His name was Noah. At some point in history, the ancestors of today's Aborigines did not transmit the true knowledge of God or the technology they once had to their offspring, and their godly legacy was lost.

It's fascinating to note that the Australian Aborigines had legends which sound like parts of Genesis 1–11. They had legends about a flood that is quite similar to the account of Noah's flood in Genesis 6 through 9. They also had creation legends that exhibited many similarities with the biblical account of Adam and Eve and the entrance of sin and death after Adam took the fruit. (This is strong circumstantial evidence that the Australian Aborigines are descendants of Noah.) After the Tower of Babel, as people groups split up and spread throughout the earth, many transmitted the history of their ancestors to coming generations. The account of the Flood was handed down, but the details changed over the years as it was passed on verbally, rather than in written form, as were the Scriptures. In the Aborigine legends, just as in the "Flood legends" of many other cultures, there are many elements similar to the Bible's account, which is the original and accurately recorded written account that has not been changed.

Sadly, however, the Australian Aborigines (as well as many other cultures) lost almost all of the knowledge they once had. I'll never forget visiting an Aboriginal mission station in North Queensland and hearing the story of an Aboriginal elder. The elder said he remembered wandering with his father as nomads across the Australian deserts. He asked his father, "What is God like?" His father replied, "I don't know, son. We've forgotten."

What a tragedy. The knowledge of God was not transmitted to the next generation — and now it was all but gone. When I spoke to the Australian Aboriginal students in my classes, in essence I was re-establishing the right foundation of thinking that had been lost for many generations.

Numerous examples from biblical history also reveal that a legacy can be lost in one generation.

For example, the Bible makes it clear that Ham committed some serious sin in regard to his father. Ham's youngest son Canaan also had some serious problems in his life, serious enough that Noah said, "Cursed be Canaan!" (Gen. 9:25). When one looks at the descendants of Canaan, we see the people of Sodom, Gomorrah, and the Canaanites — some of the most wicked people who lived on earth.

It certainly appears that Ham did not train Canaan effectively. Most likely, the same sin in Ham existed in Canaan — but to a greater extent, which often happens to the next generation. (When a particular sin in one generation is not dealt with, the same sin is often seen in subsequent generations but to an even greater extent.)

Another example of the devastation of generational compromise is found in the Books of Kings and Chronicles. As you read through Kings you are able to see the great degree of love and devotion that both David and Solomon had for God. Both kings — father and son — had a strong focus on the worship of the one true God alone. David, in particular, was uncompromising. Their devotion was demonstrated in their desire and commitment to build the great temple of the Lord.

Devastation, however, comes all too easily. Solomon's compromise started with him allowing his foreign wives to worship their pagan gods.

Then he allowed these pagan influences to infiltrate his people, resulting in them worshiping the foreign gods as well (1 Kings 11:1–4). Within one generation, Solomon's son Rehoboam made a compromising allowance for people who wanted to partake in the same idol worship in the high places. From then on, Judah spiraled further into compromise and wickedness (1 Kings 14:23). In the generation after Rehoboam, King Asa inherited the evil idolatry already in place from the previous two generations. He was a "good" king, but lacked the instruction and wisdom to eradicate this evil (1 Kings 15:11–15). The next generation was then even more distant from acknowledging this great compromise.

The compromise of Solomon and his failure to teach and lead the next generation led to a blatant disregard for God's Word. Israel had been clearly instructed not to have any gods above the One true God. Solomon's failure had disastrous effects on the worship of an entire nation for generations to come. From then on, a consistent theme runs through the Book of Kings as we read time and time again that each king continued to allow worship of foreign gods in the "high places."

Finally, at the end of 2 Kings, King Josiah rediscovered God's Word and dealt decisively with the abomination of the high places. After reading about the many consequences of ignoring God's instruction and the many warnings from godly prophets about further future consequences, King Josiah again brought Judah's focus back to the one true God alone (2 Kings 23:4–14). It is true that God was never going to be unfaithful to His commitment to Israel as His chosen people, but God did not ignore His people disregarding His instruction. A deviation of commitment to God's Word resulted in devastating consequences both for Israel and Judah for generations.

This is the overwhelmingly clear message to all of us: Humanity has never been, and never will be, able to disregard the written Word of God without major generational consequences.

Lost generations can only be restored when God's Word is again accepted uncompromisingly as truth.

The consequences of an ungodly legacy are incalculable. The repercussions send shock waves into the next generation, and even into eternity. That's why our first "component for a godly legacy" is *a compelling conviction that leads us to prioritize training up a godly generation.*

My Journey with Mally

When I was around ten years old, my parents hosted a missionary from *Open Air Campaigners* who was running a series of programs for adults and children at a nearby church. My parents widely advertised these programs and encouraged people to attend. I distinctly remember Dad and Mum picking up as many children as they could fit into the car to take them to these special outreaches. One night, I remember God instilling in me for the first time the conviction to devote my life to passing the Word of God on to the next generations.

During one of the sessions for young people, the speaker challenged us to make a decision to be a missionary for the Lord. I'll never forget the strong conviction I had to make that decision. I met with the missionary after the meeting along with a number of others. We prayed and made this very sincere commitment. I didn't know that this would mean that some 25 years later my wife and I would heed the call to leave our homeland and move to the United States as missionaries to challenge the American culture and call the church back to its foundation of the authority of the Word of God.

Like me, Mally was sent to Sunday school by her parents. One Sunday the teacher challenged the children to come forward to give their lives to the Lord. Mally knew that God had done so much for her by sending His Son to die on a cross to save her. In her heart she was willing to go anywhere and do anything her Lord wanted her to do, but being very shy, she told God that she would only go forward *if* someone else went forward, too. When she looked up, she saw that the whole Sunday school class had gone forward!

When Mally and I worked out the date this would have occurred, it was at much the same time as when I told the Lord I was willing to be a missionary for Him. The Lord was preparing *both* of us for a road ahead together . . . yet we had no inclination at the time that the other even existed. What a sovereign God we have! Little did we know what would be in store for us as the Lord took us up on our promise to serve Him!

The first time I did lay eyes on Mally, I really think it was "love at first sight." (For me at least, Mally may have had her doubts!) In January 1971, I walked into our new church in Brisbane and was handed a hymn book by this young lady welcoming people at the door. I took the book, and she took my heart, and has never given me reason to want it back. Mally too will tell you that there was something special about that first meeting, but it took some time before I captured her heart. We began meeting each other on a regular basis and in March 1972 we were engaged. We exchanged our wedding vows on December 30, 1972.

In 1976, during my second year of teaching, our first child, Nathan Robert Ham, was born in the country town of Dalby. Suddenly, we were parents. As I held that baby in my arms and looked into his face I knew that my life had new focus and purpose. I was married to a wonderful Christian wife. We wanted to serve the Lord to the utmost of our abilities. We were actively involved in the local church, and of course I was a "creation activist" at the local high school. Having my own son now, I felt profoundly different. As I replayed memories of my own childhood in my mind, thinking of how my father had invested his life in me, I began to ponder how to train up this child — the first of the next generation of Hams. What methods should we use? How could we make sure we did our best to see our children become committed Christians like ourselves? How do we ensure the biblical legacy that we have inherited continues?

As new parents, we thought long and hard about what we should do to ensure we were bringing up our children in the correct way. Again remembering how I learned from a child to build my thinking on the Scriptures, we began to develop a Christian world view in child training, one based on the Bible . . . just as my father had done before me.

Reasons for the Family

The family is the first and most fundamental of all human institutions ordained in Scripture. Steve and I praise the Lord that we were brought up in a Christian family with godly parents, knowing that many others haven't had this gift. Our faults were (and are) many, but I've often felt that our family is entrusted with a special inheritance that we need to share with others . . . *and so is yours.*

The family is the backbone of a nation.

God uses the family unit to transmit His knowledge from one generation to the next and be "salt" and "light" in the world. If the family can be destroyed, the Christian fabric in society will ultimately unravel.

The family was first ordained when God created a helper suitable for man and instructed them to be "fruitful and multiply" (Gen. 1:28). Like so many other essential doctrines of the Christian faith, the origin of marriage (and thus the family unit) finds its beginning in the Book of Genesis. Think about it: If the first 11 chapters of Genesis are not literally true, then the teaching on the family has no literal historical basis, and thus a family could be anything you wish to make it, but that is not the case. Evidence shows that the Genesis origin of the family is credible and historical.

For example, Jesus Christ quoted from Genesis chapters 2 and 3 to give the foundation of marriage and thus proclaim the true meaning of marriage (see Matt. 19:4–5). In this case, the authority of Christ gives great credence to the authority of Genesis. Jesus "created all things" (Col. 1:16). In Him "are hid all the treasures of wisdom and knowledge" (Col. 2:3). He is "the truth" (John 14:6), and He is "the Word" (John 1:1; 1 John 5:7). Jesus' authority is clear and His recognition of the authority and origin of the Genesis family is significant. The apostle Paul did much the same in Ephesians 5.

Obviously, Jesus would not quote a myth as the foundation of marriage. To do so would make marriage mean whatever you wanted it to mean, with the added consequence that Jesus would not be the truth, and the Bible would not be infallible. This is discussed in detail in various creation books and articles. (There are lists of resources and tools at the end of most chapters in this book.)

Note also that God ordained only *one* kind of family — a female mother and a male father. Mark 10:6–7 states, "But from the beginning of the creation, God made them male and female. For this reason a man shall leave his father and mother and be joined to his wife" (NKJV).

What then is the reason for marriage? What is its primary importance? Why did God make two "become one" (Gen. 2:24)? Procreation (having children) is certainly a part of the scriptural mandate that God has given to parents, and must be considered as one of the primary important reasons for marriage. With five kids of our own (and hopefully a lot of grandkids to come!) I can honestly say that my wife and I have done our part to fulfill this mandate to "go forth and multiply!" This does not seem to be the norm in our culture anymore, however.

In 1986, my wife and our four Australian children (we now have a fifth, born in San Diego) arrived on a Qantas flight into Los Angeles. As we stood up to leave the plane, someone yelled out, "Man, what a troop!" It was as if we were out of the ordinary because we had four children. In this age, many married couples are deciding to have none, one, or only a couple of children. With four, we were considered unusual. However, families with many children are becoming more common again, particularly within the home school movement and other groups within the culture. I meet home school families these days with seven, eight, and even a dozen children — I wonder what that person on the plane would have said if he had seen one of these families!

Certainly the Scripture doesn't dictate how many children a couple should have and there can be many reasons — whether medical or other — why some couples might have few or no children. However, we should all be at least aware that one of the primary purposes for marriage has not changed — to produce offspring. We certainly need to make sure we don't have a self-centered attitude when considering such matters.

It is significant that Scripture is even more specific than telling us to just have offspring; we are commanded to have *godly* offspring. In Malachi 2:15, the prophet was condemning the Israelite men for taking pagan wives:

> And did not he make one? Yet had he the residue of the spirit. And wherefore one? That he might seek a godly seed. Therefore

take heed to your spirit, and let none deal treacherously against the wife of his youth (KJV).

This passage answers the "why marriage" question directly. Why does God make two people one flesh? What is this all about? From your union He seeks "a godly seed." One of the primary reasons for marriage is to produce godly children; it is not just "seed" you are to produce, but "*godly* seed." Certainly there are other purposes for this union of man and woman, but a primary purpose for this union called marriage, which is binding and established by God in Genesis, is to have godly seed.

If we don't produce *godly* offspring, how will the future generations of the world hear the truth about living a righteous life? Romans 10:14 puts it to us this way:

> How then shall they call on him in whom they have not believed? and how shall they believe in him of whom they have not heard? and how shall they hear without a preacher? (KJV).

If godly offspring are not being produced as they used to be (as statistics indicate in our once Christianized West), could our culture end up spiritually vacant like the Australian Aborigines, or the American Indians? Not only *could* it happen, but in many parts of our culture and our world, it *is* happening. We have to look no further than Europe to see that the peoples who were once at the center of Christian strength, have now become almost entirely void of the things of God.

We must produce godly offspring, who in turn will transmit the knowledge they have to the next generation, so they will be able to transmit this to the following generation — generation after generation. It is a strategic and eternally vital task, and obviously requires considerable work to ensure information is passed on and not lost from succeeding generations.

Training That Matters

As Mally and I looked at our new son and pondered how to raise him in the things of the Lord, we were convicted by a question which has helped us develop a biblical view for bringing up our children. We challenge you to think about this question, too:

Knowing that God is the only One who knows everything and who made all things; believing that the Bible is His Word; what does God say about training children — the methods, the priorities, the nature of children, how to discipline them, etc?

If you can't answer that question, then let me ask you another question in blunt English: *Why are you having children if you don't know what God's Word teaches concerning how to raise them?* You might know what psychologists, pastors, or your parents say; but do you know what God says in His Word?

As an itinerant speaker, it is easy for me to ask pointed questions like this because I usually don't know the parents in the audience at all. It's much harder for the pastor to ask those questions because he already knows the answer, and the parents in the church know that he knows the answer, and they all know that they have to live with each other! That is why it is much easier for itinerant speakers to get away with challenging audiences in such matters, plus it's safer! I can stir them up and then get on a plane the next morning, leaving the pastor to deal with the controversy!

Sadly, from my experience traveling around Australia, the United Kingdom, and the United States, there are increasing numbers of Christian parents who are not using God's methods to produce godly offspring. On top of that, many parents don't know what the standards are by which to judge their children's behavior, so they don't know if their children measure up to godly standards. Because standards have generally dropped, many cannot see the ungodly behavior or attitudes of their offspring — they can't even recognize it. Television is a prime example. What would have been called "obscene" on television a generation ago is the norm today, and Christian parents rarely censor these programs.

Why is this so? What has happened to cause this situation? In many ways, we can use the old analogy of the "cold-blooded toad." Because a toad does not maintain a constant body temperature like a mammal, you can put it in cold water and heat it up so that the toad really does not recognize that it is being boiled to death until it is too late. We have become like the toad. We have lowered our standards to accommodate the world around us little by little, and now we can't see how much we have deviated from the standards we used to keep.[1]

The lack of a solidly biblical approach in the area of the family and education has done great harm to an entire generation of Christian children — and we are suffering the consequences in a big way. The time not spent by a father training just one child can lead to hundreds, or thousands, or millions not having the knowledge of God. (Remember the descendants of Canaan?!)

If you are a parent reading this book, do you really think you have built your thinking about child training on Scripture? Are you doing your best to train up your children to be godly offspring as the Scripture outlines for us? Could you write down clear biblical guidelines for raising your children?

Think carefully about that last question. Why not take pen and paper and see if you can answer it. If we are truly Christians, and understand that our thinking must be built on the infallible Word of God, then we should be able to write down all that God tells us about training children.

Each time I give my lecture on the family, I ask the audience to think over whether or not they could write down these things. When I do, a quiet hush comes over the auditorium, because the majority of Christian parents cannot do this! The same question can be asked of Christian teachers, Sunday school teachers, pastors, etc. If we cannot write down what God says about training children, then what right do we have to teach children or bring them into the world or make decisions or recommendations concerning their education?

Husbands and wives have all sorts of *opinions* about what a family is supposed to be, and all sorts of opinions about how to train children. But it is not a matter of our opinion; it is what God *instructs* us to do that matters. Steve and I have searched the Scriptures to obtain God's instructions and then apply them in our own families. We certainly do not have all the answers, but together we have diligently sought to use the revealed Word of God as the basis for our thinking. Our children are far from perfect, and are certainly a constant source of blessings and challenges. However, we are each proud parents of children who want to love and obey the Lord Jesus Christ with all their hearts. I am writing these pages to share with you what we have found from the Scriptures that we apply in our family daily to attempt to fulfill Proverbs 22:6:

> Train up a child in the way he should go, And when he is old he will not depart from it (NKJV).

Poodles and Priorities

I have another question I like to ask my audiences: "What are you taking to heaven with you?" Most initially respond by saying, "Nothing!" That's *almost* right. You certainly can't take your bank account, or your car, home, or boat, *but* you can take your children with you. If you are willing and committed, God can use you as a vehicle to help transport your children to heaven . . . but you have to take it seriously. Look at the following picture and then answer yet another question: Which one of these will last forever?

Which one of these will last **forever**?

We know that the car, boat, television, house, and money will all perish. What about the poodle? Sometimes children ask me if their pet dog or cat will be in heaven. I usually say, "Well, if your pet is needed in heaven, I'm sure God will make sure it is there." I know that's dodging the issue, but it's the nicest way I can think of to tell people that I *don't* believe animals continue to live on after death. Ecclesiastes 3:21 seems to hint that animals do not have immortal souls when it asks, "Who knows if the spirit of man rises upward and if the spirit of the animal goes down into the earth?" On top of that, animals were not made in the image of God, whereas humans were. So, of all the things in the picture, only the soul of the child is going to last forever.

Now observe the next picture and answer this question. Which one of these can you take with you to heaven?

Which one can you take to heaven?

The answer is obvious — only the child can be taken to heaven.

Parents, think about this: *Every child conceived in a mother's womb is a conscious being who is going to live forever and ever and ever and ever and ever and ever — in either heaven or hell.* Does that tell you something about what your priorities should be in regard to time and money? Consider this as you read Philippians 3:7–8:

> But whatever was to my profit I now consider loss for the sake of Christ. What is more, I consider everything a loss compared to the surpassing greatness of knowing Christ Jesus my Lord, for whose sake I have lost all things. I consider them rubbish that I may gain Christ (NIV).

The most important thing for anyone is that they know Christ. Nothing else ultimately matters in the big picture of things. Our lives on this earth are so short — in fact they add up to nothing compared to eternity. The car, the house, the career . . . all will vanish with time, but the soul of your child will live forever. Doesn't that make you want to take a serious look at how you are bringing up your children? Jeremiah 9:23–24 reminds us:

> This is what the LORD says: "Let not the wise man boast of his wisdom or the strong man boast of his strength or the rich man boast of his riches, but let him who boasts boast about this: that he understands and knows me, that I am the LORD, who exercises kindness, justice and righteousness on earth, for in these I delight," declares the LORD (NIV).

Once while visiting Israel, we observed the ruins of temples built by Herod I at Caesarea-Philippi, Masada, and Jerusalem. In their prime, the buildings were magnificent. Herod invested his wealth and time to leave a legacy of great buildings . . . but he wasn't at all interested in the eternal state of his soul or others. What is the result of his priorities? Herod has been dead almost 2,000 years — and now there is hardly anything left of his palaces. They are basically just a pile of weathered stones. He lived in luxury on earth, but all these material things have basically disappeared — yet Herod's soul lives on in eternity! Jesus, in Mark 8:36–37 puts the issue in perspective with these words:

For what does it profit a man to gain the whole world, and forfeit his soul? For what will a man give in exchange for his soul?

Mum and Dad were more interested in eternal matters rather than the materialism of this world. They committed their time and finances to leaving a legacy that would last forever — children who trusted Christ for salvation, who married Christian mates to produce godly offspring for the Lord. I could never thank them enough for the impact that their efforts had on me. It was an impact that was direct and eternal. Matthew 6:19–21 really sums up the difference between my parents and Herod I:

> Do not lay up for yourselves treasures on earth, where moth and rust destroy and where thieves break in and steal; but lay up for yourselves treasures in heaven, where neither moth nor rust destroys and where thieves do not break in and steal. For where your treasure is, there your heart will be also (NKJV).

What kind of legacy are you building?

Are you striving for earthly position and riches that are meaningless compared to the importance of knowing the Lord? When you are dead and your children and their children look back at your life, what kind of priorities will they see?

The Challenge Before Us

As a Christian parent, you would do well to look forward and think about your grandchildren or great-grandchildren, maybe even your great-great grandchildren. Think about this: Do you see godly offspring, or do you see generations who have not been given a godly inheritance? Within the sovereignty of God, much will depend on you.

You may need to sustain a godly heritage left by your ancestors, or you may need to start from scratch and re-create a legacy that has been lost. Either or, this is the great challenge before us:

> We are to raise godly seed by accepting our responsibilities as parents; to see our children conformed to the image of Christ,

diligently training them in truth, using the rod with love, remembering God's warnings and blessings promised – so that our children will not learn the ways of the heathen, but will be able to distinguish good from evil, and so influence the world for Christ.

That is not only a *great* challenge; it is an *important* one. The way we train our children will affect the way they train their children and so on, generation after generation. The present generation does not need to be lost. A godly legacy can be maintained; a lost legacy can be reclaimed. By the strength of grace and His Spirit in us; with the truth of His Word to instruct us, we can raise godly children in this ungodly world. The process begins with you, and you must begin with *a compelling conviction that leads you to prioritize training up a godly generation.* That is the first essential component for building a godly legacy.

Let us then search the Scriptures and determine what the biblical standards for families are and then apply them so we can train up godly seed. However, I want to warn you, as we uncover the biblical principles we are called to, you may be challenged and convicted like never before. What lies ahead is real, down to earth, and very convicting. In my plain straight Aussie English, the chapters ahead are very forthright, and to the point, and we don't pull any punches — but then neither does Scripture when it speaks on this issue! So be prepared!!

I hope you will read on with great anticipation and excitement. I trust what is written may help to change (if it is necessary) the direction your family is heading. Generations to come may be affected if you apply consistently the teachings of Scripture in this vital area.

Key thoughts from this chapter:

1. History clearly shows that an entire legacy can be lost in one generation.

2. The family is the first and most fundamental of all human institutions ordained in Scripture. It is vital as the backbone of a nation and to provide godly offspring for the next generation.

3. The consequences of an ungodly legacy are incalculable. The priority for training godly children is a multigenerational priority, and therefore it is essential that we have a multigenerational view of what we leave.

4. The first "component for a godly legacy" is *a compelling conviction that leads us to prioritize training up a godly generation.*

Questions to consider:

1. Are you aware of situations, either contemporary or historical, where a godly legacy has been lost in one generation? If so, can you pinpoint why the truth failed to be passed on?

2. How does "the challenge" make you feel? Do you feel encouraged, overwhelmed, or something else?

3. What things in your life need to be re-prioritized so that you can focus more strategically on training your children?

Endnote

1. The boiling frog anecdote has been challenged in recent times; however, the principle remains the same; http://www.answersingenesis.org/articles/rgc/godly-generations#fnList_1_1.

Ken, Malachi, and Nathan

Chapter 5

God has no grandchildren

with Steve Ham

> I know your deeds and your toil and perseverance . . . and you put to test those who call themselves apostles . . . and you have found them to be false. . . . But I have this against you, that you have left your first love (Rev. 2:2–4).

As stated in the last chapter, the first component of a godly legacy is *a compelling conviction that leads us to prioritize training up a godly generation.* Before we get too far into the "do's" of building a legacy, it is critical that you clearly understand a foundational truth of the Christian faith . . . one that is vital to your success as a parent and as a follower of Christ. *The second essential component for building a godly legacy in your children is **your** personal relationship with God through Jesus Christ.* That love relationship with our Creator is the means, the end, and the model of all you desire to pass on to your family.

It's All about Relationship

Correct teaching and consistency in discipline and instruction is foundationally important in the Christian home. It is equally important to connect this foundation with the personal and relational implications it has for our children. In his book *Beyond Belief to Convictions*,[1] Josh McDowell spends a number of chapters identifying this need. McDowell makes the following statements:

> The core of Christianity is far, far more than a set of true propositions; it is the news of a God who is passionate about His relationship with you.
>
> The incarnation says to you that despite your sin, Jesus valued you enough to die for you.
>
> You can realize your true identity as a son or daughter of your Father God who relationally accepts you unconditionally, loves you sacrificially, understands you intimately, and relates to you continuously.

Every essential biblical principle has relational truth, from Genesis to Revelation. It is truly necessary to help our children see that the authoritative biblical instruction they receive has important relational ramifications for them. For example, in relation to the incarnation of Jesus, the truth about the incarnation has massive consequences to our relationship with God. Not only is the virgin birth and incarnation of Christ *real*, but so is the *reason* for it; and the reason is a *relational* reason — one that causes us to contemplate where we stand in our *personal* relationship with Jesus as our Savior. It is not just the truth of the incarnation that is important, but the relational reason as well; and that brings me to my main point of this chapter:

God has no grandchildren.

We are all *individually* responsible to God. When saved by His awesome power, we are adopted as His personal sons and daughters. Not one of us can claim the faith of our father or mother as our own. There is no such thing as a "spiritual grandchild" of God. We each must come to Him on our own. If we don't have our own faith, we have no faith. Even though it is the same faith as others (because it is faith in Jesus), it is not *our* faith, until we own it in *our* hearts and minds. That was true for our parents; it's true for our children, and it is true for each of us.

I'm uniquely privileged to have my mother live with us in a "granny flat" (a separate living unit attached to our home). This gives my family the opportunity to pop in on a regular basis and have a chat about anything and everything. Mum enjoys it, because she misses the closeness of the relationship that she had with Dad. I enjoy it, because I regularly find out things about them that I never knew.

I recently learned about a conversation that my mother and father had before they had children. Mum sat down with my father and put forward to him that she didn't care how smart the children would be, what position in life they would have, or how they would look. No matter what, all she wanted was for them to have their own personal relationship with God. (You might think that this is a "no-brainer," but you have to understand that my father as a school principal was *very* interested in our academic grades.) My mother essentially said to him that grades and academia are unimportant compared to an individual relationship with Jesus Christ.

Ken has said, "I would rather my children be ditch diggers and go to heaven than a famous scientist or sports star and go to hell." Ken and Mally certainly believe in the value of education (they have four college graduates as children), but they know that the destiny of the soul has infinitely *more* value.

Mum, Ken, and Mally are absolutely right. *Your personal relationship with Christ must take precedence over other highly important things — even over your relationships with your earthly family.*

This is obviously a book about family heritage and family legacies —which Ken and I feel are *very* important, but it's not the *most* important thing. Our words could be misinterpreted by some as saying we can rely on our family heritage for our salvation — and this can be a trap for some. There is no doubt that God loves to save people through the avenue of family because family is His construction. We do need to know, however, that *we have nothing to boast about other than our Savior, the Lord Jesus Christ; and each of us must come to Him as an individual, regardless of our family's influence.* Paul makes this totally clear when he writes in Galatians 6:14, "May I never boast except in the cross of our Lord Jesus Christ, through which the world has been crucified to me, and I to the world" (NIV).

John the Baptist also made this brutally clear in Matthew 3, as he was preparing the way for Jesus. People from great distances were going to John, confessing sins, and being baptized. In one of the most confrontational statements said to anyone in Scripture, John turned to the Pharisees and Sadducees and rebuked them in verses 7–10:

> You brood of vipers! Who warned you to flee from the coming wrath? Produce fruit in keeping with repentance. And do not think you can say to yourselves, "We have Abraham as our father." I tell you that out of these stones God can raise up children for Abraham. The axe is already at the root of the trees, and every tree that does not produce good fruit will be cut down and thrown into the fire. I baptize you with water for repentance. But after me will come one who is more powerful than I, whose sandals I am not fit to carry. He will baptize you with the Holy Spirit and with fire. His winnowing fork is in his hand and he will clear his threshing-floor, gathering his wheat into the barn and burning up the chaff with unquenchable fire (NIV).

Apparently, certain Jews felt they held special favor with God because they had a unique religious family heritage to cling to. "We are sons and daughters of Abraham," they boasted. They misunderstood that it is *not* the family heritage that provides salvation. Salvation comes only through personal faith in our Savior Jesus Christ. (That's the *good news.*) John made it very clear to the Jewish leaders that they are responsible for their own repentance, and anyone clinging on to the faith of their forefathers, rather than accepting God's regenerating work in their own lives, will be thrown as chaff to the fire. (That's the *bad news*.)

If you are a believer and have *not* come from a Bible-believing Christian home, then you are testament to the fact that God saves from both inside and outside the family. John the Baptist looked at the pride of the Jewish leaders, called them "vipers," and then explained that God can raise up His family from the rocks. It is a clear and present warning to us all: *We are individually responsible for our faith in Jesus right now, and there is no room for boasting, except for boasting in Him and His mighty work on the Cross.*

It is important to realize that we were born into a physical legacy of sin left by our forefather Adam. Our *natural* family inheritance from Adam is one of lawlessness, suffering, and death. If you are a Christian, however, and have received Jesus as your Savior, you are now part of His *spiritual* legacy of grace, freedom, and life. If someone depends on the lineage of their physical ancestors (the lineage of Adam), only spiritual death awaits them in eternity. Those who have personally received Christ as their Savior have been adopted into His lineage (Rom. 8:14–17) and are now sons and daughters of God (in the lineage of Christ himself!).

This does not happen automatically just because you are a part of a Christian family or because you go to church or live a religious life. God created the world perfect and pure, and He created humans to rule the world in intimate fellowship with Him in harmony with all He made. Regrettably, however, Adam "fell" when he disobeyed God. Since then, men and women everywhere are born with a fallen nature that cannot do what is right. Now, each of us rejects God by doing things our own way with a rebellious, self-sufficient attitude — that is what the Bible calls "sin." In rejecting God and sinning, we make a mess not only of our own lives, but of our society and the world. God's punishment for our sin is death — the death we see all around us in the physical world and the spiritual death that separates us from our perfect Creator. Because of His love for us, God came to earth as Jesus Christ and paid for sin and death when He died on the Cross.

Then God raised Jesus from the dead to prove He had the power over death, and gave us a personal *invitation to have a* personal *relationship with Him.*

What I'm trying to say is that there needs to be a *personal* response to that invitation. It doesn't matter if you are the dirtiest heathen from a completely lost lineage, or if you come from a squeaky-clean church family. From a human perspective (knowing it is God who saves), you must respond yourself. God lays before you two ways to live:

1. You can continue living your own way, rejecting God, and trying to run your own life; resulting in condemnation, judgment, and eternal death.

2. You can submit to God and rely on the death and resurrection of Jesus Christ to pay for your sins; resulting in forgiveness, eternal life, and the receiving of God's Holy Spirit into your heart — giving you the capacity (in Him) to live righteously according to the truths of His Word.

If you have never confessed your sinfulness to Christ and received His free gift of forgiveness and grace, please consider doing so right now. We cannot overstate the eternal importance of this. A gracious, merciful Father wants to know you and live through you. An active personal relationship with Jesus Christ is to be paramount in all you do. Mum was right. A relationship with the Creator is more important than education, wealth . . . anything. It is also a prerequisite to raising godly children, lest they rightly perceive you to be a hypocrite by trying to force them to be something that you are not.

If you've never responded to His invitation, confess your sinfulness to Him now, thank Him for dying on the Cross for you, and praise Him for forgiving you. Then invite Him into your life as your Lord and Savior.

Role Models of Eternal Truth

The role of a parent is fundamentally an evangelistic one. We have been entrusted with a gift from God, and He has equipped us with His gospel. There is no greater charge to a parent than to deliver this great and momentous news. There is no greater equipping than the good and perfect revelation of God's Holy Word.

Most of all, we need to realize that we are being watched. We are the most important role models and examples our children will have on this earth. Every word and every action is being processed by those who are looking to us for guidance. We have the distinct privilege of actually showing our children how the truth of God's Word is relationally affecting our lives. In short, we get to show our children a passion for Jesus in real and relational ways.

Every time I witnessed my father picking up other children for Sunday school, I saw his passion for them to know Jesus. Every time I witnessed my father reading his Bible and in silent prayer, I witnessed his intimate relationship with his Savior. Every time I had a spiritual conversation with my dad, I was able to see how truth had personally affected his life.

Certainly, we are the most important role models of salvation to our children — yet no matter how much we apply ourselves to these biblical truths, God expects us to seek Him for the outcome in our children's lives. This is why prayer is the essential ingredient for all of these steps. Both of our parents would attribute all glory to God for our salvation. Their heart-wrenching and pleading prayers have been answered, and all six children have an individual, personal relationship with the Savior. While I am grateful for my heritage, *I was not saved by my parents*, nor were my brothers and sisters. We were saved by the gracious mercy of an all-powerful, saving God — and so were our children. All a parent can do is give themselves to Christ, diligently apply the fruit of the Spirit in their role as parents, teach and instruct according to the truth and authority of God's Word, and pray, pray, pray.

We Should Be Called the Sons of God

Matthew chapters 5–7 record the most popular sermon this world has ever heard: the Sermon on the Mount. At the beginning of this sermon are "the Beatitudes" — nine of the meatiest verses you will ever read. In these passages, Jesus taught His disciples and the masses about the fulfillment of the salvation process as the gospel is worked out in individuals' lives. In the seventh beatitude (Matt. 5:9; NIV), He teaches about the relationship between peace and being sons and daughters of God:

> Blessed are the peacemakers, for they will be called sons of God.

Nowhere in the realm of humanity can this verse be taken more seriously than in parenthood. As parents, we are the image to our children of what it is like to be a son or daughter of God. Jesus tells us that sons and daughters of God are to be peacemakers. How fitting it is to be given such a directive when we all strive to produce peaceful homes. What type of peace is Jesus talking about? In the Beatitudes, every verse is related to our condition as humans in respect to our God and the gospel. Paul explains this relationship between the gospel and peace in Romans 5:1–2:

> Therefore, since we have been justified through faith, we have peace with God through our Lord Jesus Christ, through whom we have gained access by faith into this grace in which we now stand. And we rejoice in the hope of the glory of God.

The first real peace experienced by the Christian is peace with God. Notice that Paul does not talk about having the peace *of* God or *in* God, but talks of peace *with* God. This implies that before being in Christ, we were not at peace with God, but were enemies of God and thus against God. Paul explains that we only access this peace through Jesus Christ and faith in Him alone. Faith in Christ not only reconciles us to peace with God, but also extends to us the hope of a glorious future with Him. It is this hope, worked out in our life, which brings great internal peace.

As children of God, Christ is telling us that we are responsible for being peacemakers, and that the only true peace that can be known in this world is through Jesus Christ. God the Son has reconciled us to the Father who has adopted us into an eternal inheritance. That is scriptural truth, and with that comes incredible relational realities!

This peace from God is in great contrast to the world's understanding of peace. The world is willing to seek peace with other men through a warped sense of tolerance; and then they demand that we simply accept the lifestyles and views of others. That is not something we can do. For example, if we, as Christians, tolerate the teaching of Islam, we tolerate a teaching that is at war with God. When we tolerate the homosexual lifestyle, we tolerate a lifestyle that is absolutely contrary to the design of God. When we tolerate Darwinian evolution, we tolerate a philosophy that denies God. We are commanded to attempt to be at peace with all men (Rom. 14:19; Ps. 34:14), loving them in the name of Christ, but we are never commanded to tolerate the lies that are raised up against the things of God — in fact, we are called to go to war against these lies and to *destroy* them (2 Cor. 10:3–6).

The world wants a peace, but it is an "at any cost" sense of peace . . . and they seek to find this peace through compromising God's truth. The Christian understands that there is no such thing as peace "at any cost." There is only *one* peace, and it is in Jesus Christ. We need to let the world know about this peace, as well as our Father's discipline to those that remain in disobedience. In His time, our God will bring eternal peace on this earth, and it will be at the greatest of cost to those who remain in His judgment — a judgment that will result in an eternal relational separation from God in a place where there is no peace.

Jesus tells us that peacemakers are blessed and will be called sons of God. As these sons and daughters, we need to understand the enormous task He has given us — especially as parents. In today's terms, Jesus is telling us that we will live a fulfilling and joyful life when our passion as parents is in introducing our children to the only peace they can possibly know. This is peace with God through a personal relationship with Jesus Christ, accessed only through faith in Him (not the family). As Christian parents we have been adopted by God as His children. When our children personally know God as their Heavenly Father, they too are adopted by Him, and our children then become our brothers and sisters in Christ! Our new brothers and sisters in Christ then have their own responsibility as sons and daughters of God, just as we do before Him as well.

There is no doubt that God holds the family unit in high importance. He created the family unit, instituted it, and works powerfully through it. His Word gives clear and real guidance to parents and children alike. The family is the primary unit God uses to transmit His knowledge from one generation to the next and to the world around us. He uses the Christian family and His wider church to be the salt and light of the community abroad. Yes, it is very significant that God has given you children. *Yet it is infinitely more important that our children become our brothers and sisters in Christ.* Since the parent is the strongest model in a child's life, *a parent's greatest responsibility is in being an authentic son or daughter of our great Father God.* That's the second key component for building a godly legacy, because God has no grandchildren.

Key thoughts from this chapter:

1. A parent's greatest desire should be for his or her children to have a personal relationship with the Savior. Therefore, it is essential that our children understand the relational impact of God's Word and the truth it contains.

2. No one can be saved through the faith of their family. We each have our own responsibility to know and receive Christ. This must be clearly taught.

3. The role of every parent is foundationally evangelistic to their children.

4. Worldly peace comes with compromise at great cost. The peace of God comes only through Jesus Christ and the price He paid on the Cross.

Questions to consider:

1. In what ways do you see the connection between "truth" and "relationship" being exhibited in the lives of those around you? Would you say these examples are positive or negative?

2. In modeling an authentic relationship with Jesus Christ to our children, we must believe and live what the Bible says is truth about who *we* are as His children. Contemplate the following passages:

Galatians 2:19–20

2 Corinthians 5:17

Galatians 4:4–6

1 Corinthians 3:16–17

Romans 8:1–2

How would it affect your family if they saw you truly living by these relational truths?

3. How could you convey these same truths to your children? What kind of statements could you use to communicate the truth about who they are as God's children?

Resources:

Ken Ham, *From Creation to Bethlehem*, booklet (Petersburg, KY: Answers in Genesis, 2005), 2nd printing.

Josh D. McDowell and Bob Hostetler, *Beyond Beliefs to Convictions* (Wheaton, IL: Tyndale House Publishers, 2002).

Bill Ewing, *Rest Assured Faithworks* (St. Louis, MO: Real Life Press, 2004). In this scripturally based book, biblical counselor Bill Ewing further investigates what the Word of God says is true about us as sons and daughters of God, and the phenomenal impact these truths have in everyday life.

Endnotes

1. Josh D. McDowell and Bob Hostetler, *Beyond Beliefs to Convictions* (Wheaton, IL: Tyndale House Publishers, 2002).

Ken and Dad at Kelceda St. Sunnybank Hills
— Ken had just started the creation ministry.

diligent dads

with Ken Ham

In the last two chapters, we've considered two of the three essentials needed to build a godly legacy in your home. The first was a *compelling conviction*, the second *an authentic personal relationship with Christ*. Now, in the next two chapters, we turn to a third essential component for building a godly legacy. Before you begin building, this important component must be intact:

A clear understanding of your roles and responsibilities.

This chapter will deal with the role of the father and the next chapter largely with the role of the mother — but we strongly encourage you to read them both. The perspective you will gain is very important, for the ideal situation in a family is two parents working toward the same goals in a way that complements each other's strengths and compensates for each other's weaknesses. If that is not the case, and you are doing this solo, you'll still appreciate a deeper understanding of the complete task that lies ahead. At the end of the next chapter, we will pull it all together and give you an opportunity to make a definitive commitment to leaving a godly legacy.

Much confusion exists on the topic of parental roles — and where there appears to be clarity, so often it is wrapped in so much cliché that the practical applications become lost in meaningless rhetoric. So let's cut to the quick on this vital topic, because time is of the essence.

Let me start with an idea that is both simple and profound: *God has a special plan for you.* Please let that thought soak in. *God* has a special *plan* for *you.* That is something that people have been telling me my whole life. I believe it, and I'm telling you the same now. You are not here by accident, or by chance. You are here as part of a greater plan — it's a plan God has prepared and it's a plan that involves you.

My mum has told me that when I was just a babe, a snake nearly attacked me while I sat in a stroller. Mum grabbed me and pulled me to safety. As a child, I was very sick. Several times my parents had to take me to the hospital for life-threatening emergencies that required driving through the rutted outback and forging flooded rivers to get me to help, but my mum always felt that I would be okay. She somehow knew that God had some sort of special plan for me. As a teen, my grandma (we called her Nana) also told me this, and sometimes when I would read the Bible out front in church, others would say the same. I've come to believe that God does have a special plan for me, just as He has one for you. In His marvelous Word, He has made that plan known; calling us to be *diligent dads* and *women of faith.*

Diligent Dads

Throughout the Scriptures, our special roles and responsibilities are revealed. Consider these piercing passages directed to fathers:

The father to the children shall make known thy truth (Isa. 38:19; KJV).

Fathers . . . bring them up in the nurture and admonition of the Lord (Eph. 6:4; KJV).

For I know him, that he will command his children and his household after him, and they shall keep the way of the LORD, to do justice and judgment; that the LORD may bring upon Abraham that which he hath spoken of him (Gen. 18:19; KJV).

These are just a few of the many verses that mention *fathers* in regard to training children. There is another passage of Scripture that I want you to read carefully. Note the words that are emphasized in bold:

Give ear, O my people, to my law: incline your ears to the words of my mouth. I will open my mouth in a parable: I will utter dark sayings of old: which we have heard and known, and our **fathers** have told us. We will not hide them from their **children,** shewing to the generation to come the praises of the LORD and his strength and his wonderful works that he hath done. For he established a testimony in Jacob, and appointed a law in Israel, which he commanded our **fathers,** that they should make them known to their **children**: That the generation to come might know them, even the **children** which should be born; who should arise and declare them to their **children**: That they might set their hope in God, and not **forget** the works of God, but keep his commandments (Ps. 78:1–7; KJV, emphasis added).

Psalm 78 is a long one, but I encourage you to read it through, and even write it down and keep it as a bookmark as you are studying this book. The psalm is saying over and over — *fathers,* teach your children so they'll not forget to teach their children, so that they might not forget what God has done and keep His commandments.

Sadly, in other parts of Psalm 78, we read that the Israelites *did* forget the works of God. They ended up adopting the pagan religions of the day and fell into sin because the fathers did not teach the children. One of mankind's biggest problems is forgetting what God has said or done. In the New Testament, Peter says over and over again, "I want to put you in remembrance of these things." Paul makes the same sort of statements. Why? Because God knows we are only too apt to forget.

A pastor once said to me, "My congregation has seen your videos and some went to a creation seminar a couple of years ago. Do you think they need to come to the seminar you're running in the area?" I answered, "Pastor, how many of your congregation remember what you preached last Sunday?" The pastor replied, "They'll be at the seminar!"

If you have read the Old Testament, you are familiar with the accounts of the Israelites and how God did marvelous and miraculous things for them. Sadly, though, they kept forgetting what God had done for them, and then they would complain and end up in trouble. When I read these accounts to my children, they often used to say "Dad, how come they were so stupid?! Why couldn't they remember how God took them through the Red Sea, or gave them manna from heaven, or warned them with fire from heaven? What was wrong with them, Dad?"

Well, they had the same problem we have. In fact, we are no different from the Israelites. We are only too apt to forget. How many times have we heard a great sermon at church and been convicted to apply a particular biblical principle in our lives — only to forget the principle after a few days or weeks. Then one day we hear a message on the same biblical principle and we are reminded of something we should not have forgotten. The great Psalms of the Bible begin with this admonition:

> How blessed is the man who does not walk in the counsel of the wicked, Nor stand in the path of sinners, Nor sit in the seat of scoffers! But his delight is in the law of the LORD, and in His law he meditates day and night.

Remember how the Israelites crossed the Jordan River under the leadership of Joshua? What did God tell them to do in Joshua 4:1–9? He told them to take 12 stones, from what at that time of year was a fast-flowing river, from the bottom, and build a monument with the stones, so that when their children asked, "What do these stones mean?" they would not forget to tell them what God had done.

Sadly, they do forget, and what happened with the Israelites stands as a warning for us. After Joshua and all the generation that lived with him died, the Bible records these words from Judges 2:10–13:

> And also all that generation were gathered unto their fathers: and there arose another generation after them, which knew not the LORD, nor yet the works which he had done for Israel. And the children of Israel did evil in the sight of the LORD, and served Baalim: And they forsook the LORD God of their fathers, which brought them out of the land of Egypt, and followed other gods, of the gods of the people that *were* round about them, and bowed themselves unto them, and provoked the LORD to anger. And they forsook the LORD, and served Baal and Ashtaroth (KJV).

The Israelites lost it — and in only one generation. How? Psalm 78 relates the sad event. *The fathers forgot the great works God did for them, and they obviously didn't teach the children like they should have.* Did the fathers have excuses? I'm sure they did, just like Christian fathers today who shrug off their responsibility with excuses like these: *The kids are going to church; they attend youth group; they go to a Christian school — they'll be okay.* I believe the Israelite fathers assumed because *they* knew about the great things God had done, that their children would somehow know about these things. Such acts were basically taken for granted by the fathers, and so they did not "remember" them by acknowledging them and communicating them to subsequent generations.

However, because we are born sinners, the truth needs to be taught carefully to each generation — our fallen human nature is such that we don't want truth before God saves us, and we continually struggle with the desire to sin after. Romans 3:10–11 says that "There is none righteous, not even one; there is none who understands, there is none who seeks for God." Therefore, it is absolutely vital that we continually remind our children and ourselves of the truth.

Role Reversal

Let me ask you another question I have asked of thousands upon thousands of people at seminars and meetings in different parts of the world: In the majority of Christian homes in our Western nations, is it the father or the mother who trains the children spiritually? Who really is the spiritual head of the house? Who is taking the responsibility for teaching scriptural truths to the children? Who teaches them to pray and how to act as a Christian? Is it usually the mom or dad?

You know the answer I have been given on *every* occasion I have asked this question — don't you? I'm sure you would give me the same answer! In the majority of Christian homes, it is usually the mother, not the father, who acts as the spiritual head. (In too many cases, neither the mother nor the father is fulfilling the responsibility to train their children in the things of God.) In the homes where some training is happening, the mother is usually the one that teaches, prays, and reads the Scriptures without her husband's help.

It's a reversal of God-given roles, and it's not right.

Mothers seem to be taking on the leadership roles more and more, fathers are opting out of this area all together.

This is one of the greatest problems that exist in Christian homes today. In the majority of Christian homes, it is *not* the father who is the spiritual head of, or the priest to, his family. Most fathers have neglected their biblical role as the spiritual head. They have abandoned their responsibility.

Delinquent Dads

One of the greatest travesties in our society today is that many fathers are not transmitting to the next generation the knowledge of God and His commands from the Word. What is even sadder is that most fathers don't seem to know how to do this. They don't know what it means to be the spiritual head of the house. It appears that the fathers of the past did not transmit this knowledge to the present generation and now we have a generation of fathers that has very little, if any, understanding of what the family is all about, and no one has trained them or modeled to them spiritual leadership or how to be a Christian father.

Because the legacy has been broken, men in general don't know *why* they should lead (they are missing that compelling conviction, and the significance of their God-given roles), and they don't know *how* to lead. I have had fathers come up to me and tell me that their father did not read to them or teach them or pray with them. They almost feel "sissy" doing this with their children because the strongest males in their lives didn't model any of it. Their image of masculinity is missing the spiritual component. Many Christian dads have been given no tools, no blueprint, and no materials with which to build their legacy . . . and because many know they should be leading, they are left with heavy guilt and feelings of inadequacy.

In many homes, the fathers won't (or think they can't) be the spiritual head and deliberately leave it to their wives. I do praise the Lord for the wives who take on the task to ensure their children obtain biblical training. Some wives have told me they have pleaded with their husbands to head up the spiritual training in their homes — but many times to no avail.

This is in direct disobedience to what God has clearly commanded. Dad, are you the spiritual head of your family? If not, let me warn you about something here. There are serious consequences that arise out of this neglect, and one of the graver is homosexuality. I have a good friend in Australia who ministers to men caught up in the homosexual movement. He, and others who are involved in this counseling, tells me that there is a very definite correlation between a domineering mother in the home, together with a lack of male leadership, and boys turning to homosexual behavior. (This doesn't mean that those who choose to sin in this way are not personally responsible for the decision to do so, but it does show how our parenting can contribute to the choices they make.) If we don't do things God's way, there will always be negative consequences.

As a teacher, I taught my students that the only basis for marriage was in the Bible, back in Genesis. I taught them that sex outside of marriage was against God's rules. I explained to them that marriage made them one with their spouse, just as Adam and Eve were one flesh. I showed them that God, as their Creator, had complete rights over their lives, and that if they wanted their marriage to work, they needed to obey the rules for marriage — the rules set up by the One who created marriage in the first place. Of course for Christians, I showed them from Scripture they could never even consider looking at a man or woman as a prospective husband or wife if that person was not also a Christian. I'm glad that I got to share this with my students, but quite frankly, it wasn't my job or responsibility. Teaching the children is the job of the dad. I believe that the more fathers obey the Scripture in this area, the more Christian families can be on fire for the Lord as they were created to be.

The challenge for every father is to pass on the inheritance you received from your family (if you were blessed enough to receive one), or to re-create a lost legacy if the fathers before you neglected to do so. Remember, regardless of the past, the future is your responsibility. You might have some good excuses, but the excuses end here. God says it's your job no matter what.

Remember Psalm 78? Dads, you are to be diligent to impart the knowledge of God to the next generation, period. You can easily learn to do this. We will show you how to get started shortly, but you must be committed. If you are more interested in your business or football or television; if you are giving your best to your career and come home at night too tired to even bother spending time with your children (let alone pray and read the Word with them) then you are making a big mistake. Who is really training your kids? The TV? The kids across the street? The internet? Video games and movies? Dad, don't stick your head in the sand on this one. You've only got one shot at this. Don't let the opportunity to train your children pass you by . . . the stakes are just too high for everyone.

At one church I was speaking at, a man came up to me with tears in his eyes and said, "Please, I have three children, I want to train them properly, but I don't know how. No one has ever trained me to be a father. Please can you help me?" This man (and many others) is one of the reasons I believe that the Lord has burdened us to write this book. We want to help fathers to know what God thinks about training children. The great scientist Johannes Kepler said "I want to think God's thoughts after Him." When it comes to building a godly legacy, we are wise to want to think God's thoughts as well.

You can read all sorts of books and take all sorts of classes on parenting and being a spiritual leader; but when it all comes down to it, the very most important thing you can do is

Just do it.

You are never going to do it perfectly, so you might as well just jump in and start. Here are some simple things that you can do right now that will help begin making a huge difference in your family:

1. Pray with your wife. This may seem awkward at the start, but again, *just do it.* Pray before meals. Pray in bed at night. Pray together for each of your kids as they sleep.

2. Pray for your kids. Bedtime is an ideal place to get started. When you get them tucked in, just take them by the hand and let them listen as you thank God for them and ask for His blessings on their lives. (They love that!) Ask them if they have any requests that you can pray for. In time, ask them if they want to pray out loud with you, but let them know that God always hears their silent prayers, too.

3. Study the Bible. Start reading your Bible where your family can see you. (You don't want to do this for show like the Pharisees; you do it as an authentic model for your family.) Then start reading it to them. A good place to start is Genesis 1–11 — the foundation of the rest of the Bible. Also study the Psalms or Proverbs. If it's December, start with what we call "the Christmas Message" — the babe in a manger. If it's spring (in the Northern Hemisphere), read the passages pertaining to Easter — the death and resurrection of our Savior. Start in Revelation. Start anywhere you want — but do it in a planned way — using a particular book of the Bible, or verses pertaining to a particular subject, etc. In time, let them read it to you . . . you're training them to continue the legacy with their

future family, remember? You will have a lifetime to get better at it, but most importantly, *just start NOW!*

4. Go to a good church and get plugged in. You might have to search for a while to find one that *really* ministers and teaches according to the Word of God. You might have to leave the church where you've been a member for decades, but find one that upholds the content and the authority of the Bible, and *just start going there.* (Remember, if you're looking for the "perfect" church, don't join it because you'll spoil it! There is no "perfect church" — but it is so important for the family to be a part of a local church — one that really upholds the truth of Scripture.)

Have fun and make lots of mistakes — but just do it. Because when you are long dead, will your children and children's children remember you as the spiritual head of your house who poured out sacrificial love? Will they remember that the Bible was the axiom and foundation of your home?

Be a diligent dad. Do it for the sake of your kids and future generations. It's your role and it's the right thing to do.

Key thoughts from this chapter:

1. The Bible tells us that we are, and have, forgetful children. The father of the home must constantly remind his household of God's goodness and truth.

2. Spiritual headship is the responsibility of the father. Too many fathers have become delinquent dads who are not fulfilling their God-given role.

3. Now is the time to begin. Pray with your wife and children, read the Bible together, and get involved in a good church. Take the initiative now, later is too late.

Questions to consider:

1. What kind of spiritual role models did you have growing up? How has that affected you today?

2. Is your task one of maintaining and passing on a strong spiritual legacy, or are you starting from scratch and needing to re-claim a legacy that has been long lost?

3. The most basic building blocks of being a diligent dad include prayer, Bible reading, and participation in a good church. Write down a specific plan (including times and places, etc.) for each of the areas.

Prayer

Bible Reading

Church

Forget being perfect and just do it! When you fall short or forget, just get up and do it again. In the long run, your efforts will make a huge difference.

Sarah and David playing by the family pool, ages nine and seven.

a girl named ruth

with Ken Ham

On October 22, 1971, while sitting in a car looking over the sea at a place called "Manly" in Brisbane, Australia, I asked Mally to marry me. (Can you imagine getting engaged at "Manly"?!) At the moment she said those beautiful words "I will!" neither of us had any idea of where the Lord would lead us. Many years later I realized how God had been preparing each of us for the special ministry we were to be called into, for 15 years later, in 1986, Mally and I made an important decision that would change our lives dramatically.

After visiting the United States on speaking tours, I realized that most of the churches in America did not understand the importance of the Book of Genesis, and that many had compromised with the issues of evolution and the age of the earth. I also recognized that America was the greatest Christian nation on earth, and the center of the economic world. The Lord had burdened us with the desire to see the relevance of the creation message proclaimed around the world. It was obvious that, if the creation ministry we had begun in Australia was to have a worldwide impact, we had to be active in the United States. After much prayer and seeking counsel and wisdom from others, we were convinced we had to leave Australia and begin ministry in the United States full time.

The decision was not easy. It meant leaving our family roots and saying goodbye to our homeland. It meant we would face many cultural differences and much spiritual opposition. We knew that the move would be particularly demanding and costly for Mally. Gone would be her support structure and the stability of life in familiar circumstances. Mally is considerably shy, but as we faced the decision, her strength, commitment, and devotion showed strong. She was first and foremost committed to God, willing to make great sacrifices for His kingdom. Secondly, she showed remarkable willingness to support me in the ministry I believed God was calling me to. God matched her faithfulness with His provision and a special confirmation that we were on the right track.

Toward the end of that year, we attended the wedding of one of our friends. The pastor was the father of the groom. As part of his address during the ceremony, he turned to his soon to be daughter-in-law and read from Ruth 1:8–18:

> Then Naomi said to her two daughters-in-law, "Go back, each of you, to your mother's home. May the LORD show kindness to you, as you have shown to your dead and to me. May the LORD grant that each of you will find rest in the home of another husband." Then she kissed them and they wept aloud and said to her, "We will go back with you to your people." But Naomi said, "Return home, my daughters. Why would you come with me? Am I going to have any more sons, who could become your husbands? Return home, my daughters; I am too old to have another husband.

Even if I thought there was still hope for me — even if I had a husband tonight and then gave birth to sons — would you wait until they grew up? Would you remain unmarried for them? No, my daughters. It is more bitter for me than for you, because the LORD's hand has gone out against me!" At this they wept again. Then Orpah kissed her mother-in-law good-bye, but Ruth clung to her. "Look," said Naomi, "your sister-in-law is going back to her people and her gods. Go back with her." But Ruth replied, "Don't urge me to leave you or to turn back from you. **Where you go I will go, and where you stay I will stay. Your people will be my people and your God my God. Where you die I will die, and there I will be buried.** May the LORD deal with me, be it ever so severely, if anything but death separates you and me." When Naomi realized that Ruth was determined to go with her, she stopped urging her (emphasis added).

At the time, we were making the decision to move to the United States. We were also in the process of being admitted into membership in a new church. The church we had attended moved farther out into the suburbs, so a number of members were being transferred to a different church of the same denomination.

At this new church, the pastor had a particular way of admitting new members. He would call the people out to the front and then interview them and ask them to give a short testimony about why they were joining the church.

Now Mally is a very quiet, shy person. She is not a public speaker. In fact, she is sometimes intimidated by just meeting people — she would be terrified if she had to speak to a group of people. We had been talking about this and what would happen when we were to be admitted into membership at this new church. During the wedding, when the pastor was reading from Ruth, Mally turned to me and said, "You know, I'm like Ruth. Where you go, I go. Your God is my God. I support you totally because that is what God has called me to do. How about I just say that at the church when the pastor asks for my testimony?"

A couple of weeks later, we were at our new church and the pastor called all the people being admitted into membership to come forward. Because of the unique situation of people being transferred from the other church, there were a large number of people standing at the front.

As the pastor approached people, instead of asking them for a testimony (as was his normal way of doing things), he decided he would say something about each person. He was aware of the decision Mally and I had made to move to the United States, but he knew nothing about what Mally had decided to say, and he really didn't know about the emotional struggle we were going through in regard to this decision.

When he came to Mally, he looked at her and said, "Mally, I've watched you and have known Ken's family for many years. I see how supportive you are of Ken's ministry. In thinking about you, it came to me that you reminded me of Ruth. Where Ken goes, you go. His God is your God. You support him totally in the ministry God has called him into."

Wow. To us this was a special seal from the Lord that we were making the right decision. There was such a peace in our hearts as we began the process of packing up to move to a different country. Yes, the Lord had called us to share our "inheritance" with more of the world.

The Role of a Godly Mom

Just as God made the role of a diligent dad clear, He has also made His intentions known regarding the role of a godly wife. Like so many other essential doctrines, the role of the woman is first established in Genesis:

> Then the LORD God took the man and put him into the garden of Eden to cultivate it and keep it. . . . Then the LORD God said, "It is not good for the man to be alone; I will make him a helper suitable for him." . . . So the LORD God caused a deep sleep to fall upon the man, and he slept; then He took one of his ribs and closed up the flesh at that place. The LORD God fashioned into a woman the rib which He had taken from the man, and brought her to the man. . . . For this reason a man shall leave his father

and mother, and be joined to his wife; and they shall become one flesh. And the man and his wife were both naked and were not ashamed (Gen. 2:15–25).

In the midst of our fallen world, it is important to remember that this was God's good and original design. We would do well to reclaim as much of it in Christ as we can. God fashioned a woman to complete what was lacking in Adam, that she might become his helper, that the two of them would truly become one.

Many other passages from God's Word reveal the role that God has designed for wives and mothers. One of the more pointed and all encompassing is found in Proverbs 31:10–31. (This was one of my father's favorite Scripture passages. I used to hear him quote it often in relation to his thankfulness for the gift of his wife, my mother.) The verses paint a beautiful picture of the woman God designed mothers to be. Here are some excerpts:

> An excellent wife, who can find? For her worth is far above jewels. The heart of her husband trusts in her. . . . She does him good and not evil. . . . She rises while it is still night And gives food to her household. . . . She considers a field and buys it; From her earnings she plants a vineyard. . . . She extends her hand to the poor. . . . Strength and dignity are her clothing. . . . She opens her mouth in wisdom.

These passages reveal many virtues of a woman committed to building a godly legacy for her family.

She is encouraged to be a woman of character, integrity, and action. The passages even endorse her role as a respected businesswoman in the marketplace. Certainly mothers should also be involved in teaching their children spiritual truths.

I praise the Lord for my godly mother who prayed with us when we were small, and continues to pray daily for us today, standing as my father did on the authority of God's Word. There was no doubt that Dad was the spiritual head and that our mother supported him in this role 100 percent. Whether it was cooking for visitors, supporting school functions, waiting up for Dad to return from school and church meetings — I never had any inkling that they didn't do everything together as one.

Mum also balanced out Dad in important ways. Steve remembers it this way:

> I can recall one fairly intimate chat that I had with Mum concerning our father's demeanor. She had told me of some of the many talks she had with him when he was in the process of defending God's Word. Often she would be behind the scenes persuading him and reminding him to be gentle and gracious in his approach. Sometimes Dad was about as subtle as a brick-hammer (and sometimes needed to be); yet the gentle, guiding persuasion of a godly wife was always in his ear, reminding him of his responsibility to use his words carefully and constructively. Dad had his share of faults and shortcomings, and while he allowed Mum to compensate for them in many ways, I've often felt that he could have tried a little harder to take our mother's advice. My father did definitely listen to Mum, but an even greater application of her gentle reminders would have sharpened his message.
>
> I praise God that He has also given me a wife like this — a wife who loves so much that she is willing to be honest enough to help me correct my faults in a way that will enhance and strengthen our partnership in ministry. Not only should husbands listen sincerely to their wives, but we should be seeking their input and hastening their comment. Apart from Christ, they know us better than anyone in this world!

Fathers are to be the overall spiritual head. Whenever and wherever possible, the father's leadership should be as obvious to the children as it is to the wife. The task of raising godly children in an ungodly world takes teamwork. My wife and I do this together when I am home, and Mally covers for me when I'm on the road ministering. Overall, our children know and observe that I take on the headship role and Mally takes on the helpmate role.

That is the way we were created to function, but in the modern world we often see the opposite; where the mother is leading and the dad is following. This is even reinforced by most Christian children's books I have seen where mention of spiritual leadership is made. Many of these books will picture a mother with the Bible open reading it to her children, or they will instruct the children to tell their mother something, or ask for her advice. Look closely at the books you have for your children and I am sure you will see that this is a characteristic of many children's materials available for the Christian market today.

On top of this, more women are becoming increasingly domineering as they take over the position as head of the home. The more I travel and meet families around the world, the more obvious it appears to me that the feminist movement has affected many women in our churches — and this affects the whole family structure.

We are growing up in a world that emphasizes everyone has a right to their own opinions. We are indoctrinated through the public education system and the media that we have our rights. I remember one of the female teachers at a school I taught at in Australia telling the girls in her class "Remember, if you get married, or just live with a guy, you have your rights — you are an individual." This contradicts God's design for a husband and wife to be "one," and this mindset can create serious confusion in the home.

Over the years I have observed a number of men in the Christian ministry who have had to give up the ministry, or greatly limit what they set out to do, because of an unsupportive spouse. I have also observed that some children of pastors and other full-time Christian workers rebel against Christianity. I know there are many and varied reasons for such situations. However, from my own observations and experience in traveling around the world, I do believe that one of the major factors relates very much to the fact that their wives could not cope with the husband being away or spending so much time in the demands of Christian work.

I've heard such wives question their husband's ministry in front of the children and others. The husband and wife were certainly not "one" in this regard. The wife's discontent was very obvious to the children. (It's also true that some men in Christian work have greatly neglected their wives and children, forsaking their priority to be diligent dads, and that is also a problem.) Regardless, it's important for a mom to ask: "Am I fulfilling my role as a helpmate to my husband, or am I undermining his role as the spiritual head of our home?"

The old saying is true:
"Behind every good man is a good woman."

The Ham children are blessed in heritage to be able to say that of our mother. While so many women are burdened with a heart for the superficial and material things of life, God has given a much greater responsibility; that of *supportive substance* — the type of supportive substance that is also founded and grounded in His mighty Word and shines like a beacon as an example to up and coming wives everywhere. In our case, God has provided not only a good wife and mother, but a good woman who is a mentor for women. My brother Steve has had the privilege of seeing this for himself:

> In these latter years I have had the distinct privilege of watching my mother come beside my sisters, my own wife, and younger women in the church in a soft and loving mentoring role. I've often smiled as women adopt my mother as sort of a "proxy grandma" in order to learn from her and soak in her years of experience. Mum reminds me of this passage in Titus 2:3–5:

> The older women likewise, that they be reverent in behavior, not slanderers, not given to much wine, teachers of good things — that they admonish the young women to love their husbands, to love their children, to be discreet, chaste, homemakers, good, obedient to their own husbands, that the word of God may not be blasphemed (NKJV).

There's another thing my mother is famous for — her cooking! Roast lamb, corned beef, Yorkshire pudding, exotic Aussie desserts, and much more — our mum is a chef extraordinaire! Usually when I come back to Australia to visit Mum she has my favorite cakes (like *lamingtons* — YUM!) waiting for me. Now, I know that this is unusual in today's fast-paced, microwave society. Most food today is bought in ready-to-serve packets called "TV dinners," and cakes come in boxes to which one basically adds water and cooks. I also know that there are other virtues that are more significant than cooking, but the atmosphere she created around the dinner table was a significant element in our family legacy, and my stomach is grateful!

The Biblical Ideal: Submission and Sacrifice

Consider the following from Ephesians 5:22–28:

> Wives, submit to your husbands as to the Lord. For the husband is the head of the wife as Christ is the head of the church, his body, of which he is the Saviour. Now as the church submits to Christ, so also wives should submit to their husbands in everything. Husbands, love your wives, just as Christ loved the church and gave himself up for her to make her holy, cleansing her by the washing with water through the word, and to present her to himself as a radiant church, without stain or wrinkle or any other blemish, but holy and blameless. In this same way, husbands ought to love their wives as their own bodies. He who loves his wife loves himself (NIV).

Also, carefully consider Christ's example and how Peter relates that to the roles of husbands and wives in 1 Peter 2:21–3:7:

> To this you were called, because Christ suffered for you, leaving you an example that you should follow in his steps. "He committed no sin, and no deceit was found in his mouth." When they hurled their insults at him, he did not retaliate; when he suffered, he made no threats. Instead, he entrusted himself to him who judges justly. He himself bore our sins in his body on the tree, so

that we might die to sins and live for righteousness; by his wounds you have been healed. For you were like sheep going astray, but now you have returned to the Shepherd and Overseer of your souls. **Wives, in the same way be submissive to your husbands** so that, if any of them do not believe the word, they may be won over without words by the behavior of their wives, when they see the purity and reverence of your lives. . . . **Husbands, in the same way be considerate as you live with your wives**, and treat them with respect as the weaker partner and as heirs with you of the gracious gift of life, so that nothing will hinder your prayers (NIV; emphasis added).

Both husband and wife are called to model their lives after Christ, and He was submissive to the point of death on the Cross.

That is some submission! Women should "in the same way" be submissive to their husbands. Husbands are to "in the same way" love their wives. That is some sacrificial love a husband is to pour out on his wife! As it states in Ephesians 5:25, "Husbands, love your wives, even as Christ also loved the church, and gave himself for it."

Maybe if husbands loved their wives like this (with a sacrificial love), their wives wouldn't have a problem with godly submission. Maybe if wives were submissive to their husbands (with a sacrificial submission), they wouldn't have problems with husbands loving them as they should.

Dad and Mum may have had disagreements at times, as all couples no doubt do, but I cannot remember them having any fights in front of us. I remember them as a couple devoted to each other. They clearly showed they loved us and they did what they should to train us up as godly offspring. What an example they were to us! I believe that such stability and obvious outworking of obedience to the Scripture by our parents had a major impact on all of us children — all who today have stable marriages where husbands and wives are totally devoted to each other. I could not even imagine what it must be like to have been brought up in a home without such stability, love, and devotion — and I can't help but wonder what sorts of issues marriage problems cause in the next generation.

The point is this: *Both husbands and wives need to be obedient to what God says*, and not their opinions or feelings! That is God's ideal design for the family, but we do live in a less than perfect world because of sin and the curse. We have families that have mothers and fathers that cannot (or will not) fulfill their God-given roles. We have orphans. We have foster kids. We have widows and widowers. Single parents and those dealing with broken marriages have a very complicated and difficult task before them . . . and I believe God gives a special measure of grace to men and women in these sad situations. Those of us who are aware of such families need to do whatever we can to support them and maybe even be role models for their children. These are the times when the Body is to work as a body, healing, supporting, and compensating for other parts of the body that are in need.

When Mally and I were making our decision to come to the United States, it was very difficult to consider leaving family and friends. We agonized over the decision day after day. Luke 14:26–27 says, "If anyone comes to me and does not hate his father and mother, his wife and children, his brothers and sisters — yes, even his own life — he cannot be my disciple. Anyone who does not carry his cross and follow me cannot be my disciple." We knew what we needed to do, but we also knew that it would leave a big hole in our extended family, particularly with me being on the road so much.

When we moved to San Diego in January of 1987, it was hard to make friends and learn how to live in a country that has many cultural differences; but God knew what we needed. The house we purchased "just happened" to be next door to a wonderful older couple who became "Grandma Jo" and "Poppa Bill" to our children. What a blessing! God was looking after us in special ways. Poppa Bill has left this earth now, but Grandma Jo is still Grandma Jo to our kids in the United States, and they are an excellent example of how God provides for a family unit through the larger body of Christ.

Let's be honest. We live in a fallen world and the perfect family doesn't exist. There are many families out there that need us to help them be whole and healthy. It's much easier to condemn and judge others for the circumstances they are in (often by their own making), but isn't this an opportunity for us, as members of Christ's body, to minister to others in His name? Isn't this an opportunity for us to be vulnerable and admit that we too need the help of others around us?

Poppa Bill and Grandma Jo filled a big spot in our hearts, but the move was still very difficult on Mally. She never complained, but I knew she was still lonely and greatly missed family. We prayed about this, and the Lord answered in a way we didn't expect. He gave us a baby daughter! What a special gift this was for all of us, particularly Mally.

As we thought about this answer to prayer and why we were in the United States, we decided to name our daughter Kristel Ruth Ham. She is a reminder to us of the seal that the Lord put on our ministry in the United States — and more than that, her name is a continual reminder to me that Mally is like Ruth, a submissive, devoted wife whom I continue to fall in love with day after day!

Mally has said to me many times that she sees her role is to support me in whatever way she can so that I can carry out the ministry God has called me to be actively involved in. This has often been demanding and taxing on her, requiring that she fill in for me when I'm gone. (I don't know why, but it always seems that the washing machine waits to leak or the heater decides to blow when I'm away.) Usually, Mally never mentions these things to me; she doesn't want problems at home to detract from the ministry I'm involved in.

Her attitude was obvious to our children. There is no doubt in their minds at all that their mother supports their dad 100 percent. I believe this has had a lot to do with why our children have not rebelled against my absences and the reason why they are so supportive (just like their mother) of the itinerant creation ministry I am actively a part of.

I could write an entire book about how Mally has been the best helpmate I could ever have. I love her more every day and could not even express in words how much I appreciate her and love her as a wife. She is also a wonderful mother and grandmother — always putting others first and herself last. When it comes to Answers in Genesis, Mally has made all the difference in the world — and I mean that literally: The world is different because of her. I seem to get so much of the credit, but let there be no doubt that God uses Mally and the gifts and strength He has given her in amazing ways. He has used her sacrifice and support (as well as her willingness to put up with my faults and cover for my weaknesses!) to make this ministry what it is.

I'm truly blessed by the Lord every time I see committed, godly parents — those who are living according to the roles given us in the Bible. Mally also rejoices in parents who are totally committed to the truth of Scripture and display this to their children. When parents choose to obey God and fulfill their God-given roles as described in Scripture, God's grace and blessings abound to all around and He is glorified.

As Steve and I look back at the legacy left by our father, there is no doubt that Mum's presence was a definitive factor in the inheritance he was able to leave. The godly leadership of my father was evident in the way my mother loved and supported him in return, as well as in the way she endlessly cared for us children. Since Dad's passing, she has also had her fair share of health issues, including cancer. I have witnessed my brothers and sisters rally together in assisting Mum to sell her home, move her into a granny flat built on Steve's house, and constantly care for her needs. I interpret this as the gratitude we all have for the biblical heritage Mum and Dad have striven so hard over the years to supply. In fact, we see it as a true privilege and service not only to our mother, but our Sovereign Lord.

These words will undoubtedly make Mum uncomfortable. She will be the first to point out that any good in her comes not from herself, but from the work of God in her and through her. Like the rest of us, she is made of sinful flesh; but she has also chosen to submit to the Word of God and the Holy Spirit. His truth and His presence in her have accomplished holy things. She has been and continues to be a supportive substance, a gentle but strong balancing presence, a defender of truth, a godly trainer of her children, and a powerful mentor of women in the Lord.

Mum may also have difficulty with these words because she has never been one to seek out or expect recognition or praise. But sorry, Mum! It is only fitting. At the end of the description of an excellent wife in Proverbs 31, it says:

> Her children rise up and bless her; Her husband also, and he praises her saying: "Many daughters have done nobly, but you excel them all." Charm is deceitful and beauty is vain, But a woman who fears the Lord, she shall be praised (Prov. 31:28–30).

Let God's Word be proven true again!

Key thoughts from this chapter:

1. Wives and mothers have an important role of support in the home. This role is described in Genesis 2, Proverbs 31, and many other places in Scripture.

2. In our fallen world, role reversal is common and unfortunate. Believers should seek to minister to those who are living in less than ideal circumstances.

3. Submission and sacrifice is the model given to wives by Christ. Love and sacrifice is the model Christ gives to the husband.

4. Supporting the strong Christian leadership of a godly father is the strongest adhesive a wife brings in building a biblical legacy.

Questions to consider

1. Why do you think both husbands and wives avoid their responsibility to fulfill their God-given roles?

2. What are some of the consequences you have observed when roles are reversed?

3. Prayerfully consider the passages quoted above from Genesis, Proverbs, and Ephesians. In what specific ways do you need to be obedient to the commands of God in these passages?

Pulling it all together

In the last four chapters we have presented the three essential components for building a godly legacy: 1) *a compelling conviction that leads us to prioritize training up a godly generation;* 2) *your personal relationship with God through Jesus Christ;* and 3) *a clear understanding of your roles and responsibilities.*

Each of these components is necessary. If you try to build the legacy without even one of them, it will not last. None of these components will lead to a godly inheritance for your children unless you actually *commit* to acting on them . . . and that can be difficult to do if you feel like you must implement these components on your own. Thankfully, that is not the case. Consider these two passages:

> Abide in Me, and I in you. As the branch cannot bear fruit of itself unless it abides in the vine, so neither can you unless you abide in Me. I am the vine, you are the branches; he who abides in Me and I in him, he bears much fruit, for apart from Me you can do nothing (John 15:4–5).

> I can do all things through Christ who strengthens me (Phil. 4:16; NKJV).

The three components are essential, and the commitment must be yours, but your real challenge is to be dependent on Him to fulfill the very things He commands you to do. Understanding this will give you strength when times are tough, and ensure that He gets the glory for all the blessings.

If you and your spouse are "one" in the matters we have written about in the preceding chapters, we would invite you to come together and make the following prayer of commitment as husband and wife. If you are a single parent or you must build a legacy without the support of your mate, we invite you to make this commitment as well, knowing that God himself will be your partner as you endeavor to raise godly children in this ungodly world.

Our God and our Creator,

We come to You now with empty hands, recognizing that all we are, and all we have is a gift from You. You have made all things, and nothing has come into being that You have not made. We praise You for the children You have entrusted to us, and we deeply desire to build a godly legacy that will be a blessed inheritance to them, to their children, and to the generations to follow.

It is clear that Your Word, and only Your Word, can be the foundation for this legacy. The empty opinions of man and the fallible wisdom of the world can never be a substitute for Your perfect and living Word. Give us the willingness to search the Scriptures to discover the principles and commands that You have given us to obey.

Father, we humbly fear that the knowledge of You can be lost in a single generation. By the truth of Your Word, and by the power of Your Spirit, we ask that You will instill in our hearts a compelling conviction that leads us to prioritize the task of training up a godly generation. Increase our love for You in our personal relationship with You through Jesus Christ, so that we might be an authentic model to our children, and that we might be empowered in our tasks by the very presence of You in our hearts. Give us a clear understanding of the roles and responsibilities You have created us to fulfill.

Our sinful tendencies will try to lead us into disobedience to Your will. We know that without You, we can do nothing, but that through Jesus Christ, we can do all things. Lord, we place ourselves humbly in Your hands. Use us as You see fit to be sacrificial, submissive, and loving to each other and to our children; that we might be used to build a godly legacy and leave a rich spiritual inheritance that brings glory, honor, and dominion to You and You only.

Amen

PART 3:

BUILDING
A LEGACY

Unless the Lord builds the house,
They labor in vain who build it
(Ps. 127:1).

Our Lord and our God,

As we now turn our attention to the task of building our homes into an environment for sanctification, as we seek to leave behind a godly legacy, as we strive to raise godly children in this ungodly world, we ask for Your direction, Your strength, and Your guidance. The task is so monumental and so overwhelming that we now turn to You, for there are many things that we can't do at all. You alone are the One who can build our homes; You alone are the One who can change hearts. You alone are the One who can give us courage, wisdom, and commitment.

We entrust it all to You now, asking that You alone would be the One to receive glory and honor.

Amen

Trish, David (10), Sarah (12), and Stephen
in the family home, April 2006.

CHAPTER 8

creating the environment of sanctification

with Stephen Ham

There is a time for everything,
and a season for
every activity under heaven:
a time to be born
and a time to die,
a time to plant
and a time to uproot
(Eccles. 3:1–2; NIV).

Polaroid Babies

Let's be honest: It's a lot easier to make babies than it is to raise them — at least from a male's perspective, that is! There is no better example of this than my brother Ken. Over the span of a dozen years, he and Mally had five beautiful children. We called them "Polaroid Babies," because it seemed they could deliver children at the press of a button.

Ken's firstborn came into the world on November 10, 1976, in the rural town of Dalby, Queensland, in Australia. Mally had been in labor almost seven hours, but a lot of this was because of the size of Nathan's head. The doctor warned them that the baby had a large hematoma. Nobody was quite sure what that was, but it made his son look like he had two heads for a while. Oh well, like they always say, "Two heads are better than one." His baby pictures were cute though, and Nathan has grown into a fine man.

On February 22, 1978, Mally went into labor with their second child . . . and #2 sure knew how to make a grand entrance. Mally sensed right away that they needed to get to the hospital *now*. Ken tried counting contractions (you know, like a good husband is supposed to) but he couldn't count fast enough and called the ambulance in a somewhat panicked state . . . and of course the person who answered tried to be calm asking, "Mr. Ham, is this your first or second? How far apart are the contractions?" Ken blurted out something to the effect that what was happening wasn't normal and they needed to get there immediately. He was told, "Yes, Mr. Ham, we'll send someone. Just stay calm." They didn't believe him, so Ken took the issue to the top and called on Mum!

When Mum took one look at the situation, she knew the baby was well on the way. She had six of her own, but had never been on the receiving end of a delivery. She ran for the kitchen to make preparations. Ken was stressed out of his mind, praying like he had never prayed before, hoping the ambulance would show up. That's when Mally called for him. He raced to her side to see the baby's head appearing. He grabbed the baby as it delivered. Again relying on his vast medical experience gained from the movies, Ken held the baby by the feet and spanked it — and the baby started to cry, just like it was supposed to. Then he remembered seeing doctors clean out the baby's mouth, so he put his finger in its mouth and kind of moved it around, hoping it cleared whatever it was supposed to.

Again Ken remembered hearing that people have used their boot laces to cut the umbilical cord, so he pulled out his boot lace and then stood there, without a clue of what to do next. Right at this time, a lady that Mum had called rushed in. She was trained as a midwife and calmly took over. She took the bootlace and tied the cord, and prepared Mally for the ambulance. As the paramedics walked up the stairs, Ken handed them a baby, mumbling something about the fact that they should have believed him!

At the hospital, one of the nurses asked Ken, "So, is it a boy or girl?" Ken embarrassingly replied, "I don't know, I forgot to look!" After they checked, they named her Renee Elizabeth. Mally was in labor for only 45 minutes, and we'll never know for sure if this had some sort of lasting effect on Renee — but she became a nurse and learned how to deliver babies!

Mally and Ken were so sure that #3 would be a boy that they named him Daniel ahead of time. He saw the light of day after only 40 minutes of labor . . . but after one look, they decided to name "him" Danielle instead.

Child #4 came in 1984. On September 29, Mally told Ken that it was time. Ken called the ambulance company, who (now well aware of the history of the Ham family) made it to the door in about 17.3 seconds. Still, Jeremy was born halfway to the hospital, only 11 minutes after the first contraction. He delivered in the back of an ambulance early in the evening, under a tree overlooking the city of Brisbane. Ken told Mally, "At least you had a nice romantic view of the city while he was being delivered!" (Mally didn't seem to appreciate that comment for some reason.)

On February 25, 1988, while in Chicago preaching at a church, Ken was given a note telling him that #5, Kristel Ruth, had been born. This sort of interrupted the service, as you might imagine! Ken would have liked to have been there for that birth, of course, but Kristel only gave them 38 minutes of warning and Ken was about two thousand miles away.

It's certainly humorous to look back on all this and reminisce about Ken and Mally's exciting births. I would love to tell you lots about the birth of my own children, but during both births I was using all my own concentration and a lot of assistance from the nursing staff just to keep my dinner down and prevent myself from fainting. Both Sarah and David arrived safely into the world despite my wife's poor excuse for a supportive husband. I am just glad that Trish talked me through the labor and kept me concentrating on my breathing.

Inducing the Environment for Sanctification

Yes, some kids are relatively easy to deliver, but all are a challenge to train. We've established that the Word of God is the one and only foundation of a godly legacy. We've seen that *compelling conviction, a personal relationship with Christ,* and *a clear understanding of our roles and responsibilities* are the three essential components needed to leave a godly inheritance for the generations to come. As we now turn our thoughts to the "how to's" of training godly children, we must realize that one of our primary goals is to *orchestrate a household atmosphere for sanctification.*

Sanctification is the ongoing process of becoming more like Christ (an entirely different process than secular "behavior modification"). It's important to acknowledge that sanctification only happens through the power of the Holy Spirit, yet an environment focused on the correct teaching and application of God's Word is an environment that is consistent with the Holy Spirit's work. If our God is truly sovereign and all knowing, surely His instruction is supreme and sufficient to guide our family into this holiness!

God's good and perfect truth is revealed to us in His amazing Word. As we established in Part 1, that is the foundation — the rock-solid base for building a godly legacy. So how do we build upon this foundation? How do we create an environment for spiritual growth?

> ### By communicating to our children both the content of the Bible and the authority of the Bible.

Building with the Content of the Bible

In many homes, a Bible is a symbol of religion. Like an icon, it sits on the shelf representing some sort of affiliation of spiritual devotion. This was never what the Word of God was intended to be. Hebrews 4:12 says:

The Word of God is living and active and sharper than any two-edged sword, and piercing as far as the division of soul and spirit, of both joints and marrow, and able to judge the thoughts and intentions of the heart.

The Bible is God's message to humanity and the family. The message is alive, and the meaning of that message is essential to everyone who desires to create an environment of sanctification in the home. The communication of truthful biblical *content* is non-negotiable.

The apostle Paul clearly understood and enunciated this in his writings. Throughout the Epistles, Paul gives a number of instances where false doctrines have affected the Church. Consider 1 Timothy 1:3–7. Look closely at this passage as Paul, under the inspiration of the Holy Spirit writing the infallible Word of God, confronts the clash of false biblical teaching with purity, conscience, and faith:

> As I urged you when I went into Macedonia, stay there in Ephesus so that you may **command certain men not to teach false doctrines** any longer nor to devote themselves to myths and endless genealogies. These promote controversies rather than God's work — which is by faith. **The goal of this command is love, which comes from a pure heart and a good conscience and a sincere faith.** Some have wandered away from these and turned to meaningless talk. They want to be teachers of the law, but they do not know what they are talking about or what they so confidently affirm (NIV; emphasis added).

In this passage, Paul exhorts Timothy to deal head-on with false doctrines, because such doctrines are incompatible with love, a pure heart, good conscience, and a sincere faith.

Note the connection between love, purity of heart, clarity of conscience, and sincerity of faith. These things are impacted by *truth* and the basis for truth, which is sound doctrine. The very position Paul comes from is a position of love abounding in purity, good conscience, and sincere faith. Because of this position, there is no room for the tolerance of false

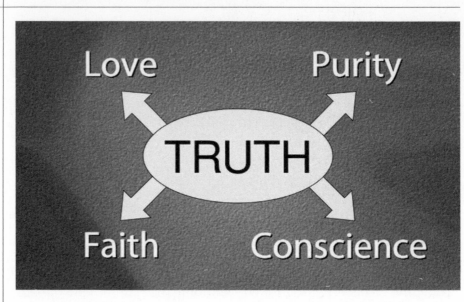

teaching. It stands to reason that sincerity of faith, purity of heart, and good conscience are only compatible with truth, and that truth only comes from the actual words of Scripture. Thus, a compromise in truth compromises love, purity, conscience, and faith.

As Christian parents, our love for our children is enormous. I am sure that the last thing we want is for our children to have a dented, stunted, or non-existent faith. Faith comes from God, yet we must also acknowledge that we have been given a responsibility to provide a growing environment for strengthening the faith. A loving parent surely has a desire for their household to be a growing environment for sanctification, one that is built on the authority of God's Word.

At this stage we shouldn't overlook a very important point:

For our children to grow in a strong basis for the belief and defense of Scripture (and thus a strong basis for their faith), they need to be taught that the content of Scripture is real, not just symbolic or illustrative.

One of Ken's pet hates is the concept of "Bible stories." Parents and Sunday schools around the world are innocently teaching children what we

call "Bible stories," normally illustrated with unrealistic childlike illustrations. Noah's ark, for example, is typically shown as a beautifully drawn little overloaded boat showing animals with their smiling faces hanging out the windows. However, nearly all of these "arks" would potentially sink at the first sign of water, let alone the oceanic turmoil the true ark faced during the Flood. Also, these chubby little boats are not even close to the size required to fit all the animal kinds on board. . . . I guess that's why the animals always have to poke their heads out of the windows!

A realistic-looking ark

Now some of you are probably saying, "Come on. It's okay, they're only kids!" The sad fact is that the statement is true! They *are* only kids — kids that are vulnerable, teachable, and open to influence from us — and everyone else. Many don't seem to realize children are *very* impressionable and open to *every* influence from the world. They are susceptible to every destructive, Bible-doubting idea around. When we present God's Word as "stories" and illustrate them in a way that gives the impression they are a fairy tale, can a child differentiate between Scripture and Aesop's *Fables*? I don't think so. When will we start becoming serious about teaching our children biblical *truth*, instead of biblical *tales?* Keep in mind that the world scoffs at the account of Noah's ark and the worldwide Flood — such fairy tale looking arks actually help them scoff.

My father carefully constructed a scale model of the real ark from the dimensions given in the Bible. It is a beautiful piece of work, meticulously re-created and crafted. Dad certainly wanted to ensure that people understood that the content of God's Word could be trusted; and we need to do the same. *Never present the Bible as anything less than it is: The living Word of God.* The main point is that as we were taught content, we were also taught the *trustworthiness* of the content and that the content was real. Dad always reminded us that the message was from God and that the Bible dealt with objective truth.

Certainly there is a place for children's stories, symbolism, and allegory in our training. The fictional works of C.S. Lewis and John Bunyan are excellent examples, but whenever you open the Bible, make sure that your children understand that the content of this book is *real*. When it comes to holidays, make sure that your children understand that there is no correlation between the reality of our Savior Jesus Christ and the fictional Santa and Easter Bunny, etc. Trish and I have never used Santa Claus in any part of our family Christmas celebrations so that we don't cause confusion in this area.

An environment for sanctification cannot happen without the *content* of the Word being regularly communicated as truth to the child. At the same time, please know that *faithfulness* and not *perfection* is the key to effectively communicating the content of Scripture. I asked Ken and Mally what they did in regard to teaching biblical truths to their children. They told me this:

> Devotions in our home have never been perfect. We just called it "Bible time." The kids got used to it and came to love it. When they were little we would start with a good picture Bible, and tell them the history and details of what was going on in the pictures. As they got older, we would read to them from the Word, and then have them read to us.
>
> As they grew, it became more than just reading the Bible, it became a time to communicate a biblical world view. We read books like *The Pilgrim's Progress, Leading Little Ones to God*, and a fictional series called *Minni and Maxie Muffin*. It was a great time, and we all learned a lot. It also made a statement. Every time we had Bible time, it communicated that the Book we held in our hand was important.

My own children (David and Sarah) have become competent readers, and we strongly encourage them each night to have their own "Bible time." We assist them by providing study aids that can help them investigate the Bible for themselves . . . but we are always extremely careful when it comes to such material. We have had some significant conversations with our daughter about the extra-biblical comments in the margins. This careful monitoring of biblical aids has helped us teach our children discernment and helps them understand that there is *no* substitute for the Word of God. If you are looking for trustworthy material to help your children develop their own devotional habits, I recommend a book called *A Faith to Grow On*, by John MacArthur.

Again, strive to be *faithful* and *not perfect* as you train your children in the Word. If you think you are going to organize in-depth exegetical surveys of Scripture and keep it up on a systematic schedule, you are probably mistaken. (Or you will feel so overwhelmed that you won't even attempt anything.)

The key is to set some time aside on a somewhat regular basis so you can share the content of Scripture with each other.

Over the years, these humble efforts will have a significant impact on your heart and the souls of your family.

Building with the Authority of the Bible

Creating an environment of sanctification in a home requires that we communicate the *authority* of the Bible as well as its content. When it comes to children (and everyone else for that matter), a truth-driven and authoritative foundation is of the utmost importance. Remember, we are relying on God's Word to establish a basis for faith, and not some unsubstantiated idea.

When we want our children to acknowledge faith in God, they must also acknowledge the authority of that God. Therefore, as we read God's Word to them, we must read from an authoritative position. When we display the truth and authority of Scripture, it will help our children see the curse of sin in the inaccuracies of this world's teachings, and the fallible and corrupt nature of man.

It is therefore imperative that we have a good understanding of the essential doctrine of "The authority and inspiration of Scripture." Consider God's words in 2 Peter 1:19–20:

> And we have the word of the prophets made more certain, and you will do well to pay attention to it, as to a light shining in a dark place, until the day dawns and the morning star rises in your hearts. Above all you must understand that no prophecy of Scripture came about by the prophet's own interpretation. For prophecy never had its origin in the will of man, but men spoke from God as they were carried along by the Holy Spirit.

The very definition of the word "authority" is "*the right or power to require obedience.*" Peter plainly asserts that Scripture came about not by men under a light influence of God, but by men *completely* under the influence of God in the direction of *every* word. If every word is God's Word, then every word is authoritative — and every word in every subject.

Dr. Martyn Lloyd-Jones is known as one of the most influential evangelical leaders of the previous generation. He was also a great model of Christian parenting. (I highly recommend the reading of his biography, *A Family Portrait*.) In a series of lectures on evangelicalism entitled *What Is an Evangelical*,[1] he said:

> The basis of faith says, "We believe in the divine inspiration and entire trustworthiness of Holy Scripture as originally given, and its supreme authority in all matters of faith and conduct." I contend that it is not enough just to say that; we have got to go further. There are people who claim to subscribe to that doctrine, who, I would suggest, in some of their statements raise very serious doubts as to whether they really do accept it.
>
> So we have to say some specific things such as that the Scripture is our **SOLE** authority, not only the supreme authority, but our sole authority, our only authority.
>
> Then the next thing to be said under this heading of scripture is that we must believe the whole Bible. We must believe the history of the Bible as well as its didactic teaching. . . . Today there are men who say, "Oh yes, we believe in the Bible and its supreme authority in matters of religion, but, of course, we don't go to the Bible for science; we go to it for help for our souls, for salvation, and help and instruction in the way to live the Christian life." They are saying that there are, as it were, two great authorities and two means of revelation: one of them is Scripture and the other one is nature. These, they say, are complementary, they are collateral, and so you go to the Scriptures for matters concerning your soul, but you do not go to them to seek God's other revelation of himself in nature. For that, you go to science. . . .
>
> Their argument was that they were merely out to defend the truth of the gospel against this natural science — and let us grant that their motive is good and true. Our friends today are doing

exactly the same thing. It seems to me that in so doing they are on the path that always ends in the same result, namely that the gospel itself is compromised. We must assert that we believe in the historicity of the early chapters of Genesis and all other biblical history.

To create a godly environment of sanctification, we have to stand with men such as Dr. Martyn Lloyd-Jones and teach and defend the authority of the Bible in regard to every word. If we allow teaching that compromises the authority of God's Word to infiltrate our household, we essentially compromise the sanctifying environment of our homes. We need to let our children see us taking this stand, even against high-profile Christian leaders if necessary, to honor God and show that we are serious about a strongly substantiated faith in Him as Almighty Creator.

This doesn't mean that we are all to be like Pharisees, just looking for legalistic arguments around points of law. In fact, an adherence to the authority of God's Word would have us understand that abstract legalism is harmful.

Our father would often read commentaries to allow other God-fearing men to help him to a deeper understanding of Scripture, but the Bible was always his sole source of truth. Especially when it came to essential doctrines, my father would often point out to me where a particular author's statements did not correlate with Scripture. This was a dual defense on his part. He was defending the content of the Word and the authority of God's Word by showing that man's words and opinions were subordinate. In doing so, he was also defending our household against humanism, mankind's fallible nature, and their attacks on our home. That is why my father often said to me, "The Bible is a great commentary on commentaries."

Faith substantiated by the Word is essential. Every time our children walk out the front door of our home, the world is waiting to attack their faith. Even inside our homes, television sets are constantly telling them that biblical truth does not match modern science. Even many Christian schools and Christian resources teach our children humanistic principles that point to the Bible as an untrustworthy source of information.

From Paul's teaching, we have clearly seen that the content and authority of Scripture is inseparably linked to the issues of love and faith. Yet, we need to ask a question: How many households of good Christian intention are building an environment of sanctification with these things? The foundation of the Word of God is the beginning of a home built on the content and authority of that Word. God created it that way in love for the good of the faith in our children.

This is where I get to stand with all of my brothers and sisters, and say how blessed we were to have parents that not only had good intentions, but backed them up by standing on the authority of the Word of God. They taught not only the content of the Word of God to us, but also continually helped us to see the authority of the content.

As the youngest in my family, I had the added benefit of being influenced by the ministry of my brother Ken from a very early age. My earliest memories are of being taught logical and consistent answers to the world's attack on my faith. Sadly, many of these answers had to be used against attacks from within the church.

Our Dad's Example Prevails

Everyone who knew our father well will remember walking up the front stairs of our home and looking through the screen door to see him in his favorite chair. The chair had been given to him as a retirement gift after he left his education career for health reasons, and he sometimes spent the better part of the day sitting, reading, praying, and thinking in it. He usually had his Bible in his hand or open on his lap. Often he would be speaking softly to himself, reinforcing the truths he was learning. I can even hear his whispers now. Those whispers are whispers God used to save my life. Dad focused on the environment for sanctification in our house, starting with a focus on sanctification in his own life.

Dad was passionate about me knowing the truth of Jesus. Often I would sit across from him as he sat in that old chair. I can almost still hear his voice as he spoke the same words Solomon spoke to his son, "Listen to me. Listen to wisdom." He wasn't just trying to get his point across; he wasn't trying to manipulate me to modify my behavior. He wanted me to hear the Word of God. I am so glad that even when I didn't want to hear it, he told me anyway . . . because that teaching is what God has used to bring me into a closeness with Him — a closeness that I now experience nowhere else.

My father never took a parenting course. He knew that the courses and theories of man come and go. Instead, he gave me something that would last forever:

He gave me authoritative instruction from the Bible, and allowed me to view Christ in him.

That was the best environment for my sanctification that I could ever imagine.

Key thoughts from this chapter:

1. Building a legacy requires providing an environment where your children can meet and grow in maturity in Christ.

2. An "environment for sanctification" is built by communicating the *content* and the *authority* of the Bible.

3. The content of Scripture must be presented as being real.

4. The authority of Scripture must be presented as being absolute and all encompassing.

5. Maturing in faith, purity, and conscience is directly co-related with truth. Without a foundation, truth, faith, purity, and conscience are compromised.

Building blocks:

1. Always delineate between fact and fiction when reading to your children, making sure that the Bible's history is presented as truth.

2. Talk about scriptural truth in normal conversation, ensuring your children understand biblical reality and its impact on day-to-day living.

3. Regularly spend time with them discussing scriptural truth through devotions, what they learned in Sunday school, or from their friends. You will be amazed at what a scriptural view will open up for them and correct what they have already heard!

4. Work out a flexible strategy to communicate both the content and the authority of God's Word faithfully, not perfectly!

5. When appropriate, allow your children to view you as you study, teach, and defend the Bible.

Questions to consider:

1. Consider Paul's exhortation to Timothy: ". . . command certain men not to teach false doctrines. . . . The goal of this command is love, which comes from a pure heart, and a good conscience and a sincere faith" (1 Tim. 1:3–5). Where have you seen false doctrine interfere with love, conscience, and faith?

2. In what settings have you experienced both the content and the authority of Scripture being communicated? Would you say these experiences are the exception or the norm?

3. In what ways can you, as a parent, build a stronger environment for sanctification in your home?

Resources and tools:

Christopher Catherwood, *Martyn Lloyd-Jones: A Family Portrait* (Eastbourne, UK: Kingsway Publications, 1995).

John MacArthur, *A Faith to Grow On* (Nashville, TN: Tommy Nelson, 2000).

Endnotes

1. D. Martyn Lloyd-Jones, *What Is an Evangelical?* (Edinburgh, UK: Banner of Truth and Trust, 1992).

Ken and Mally's first grandchildren, Malachi and Kathryn

CHAPTER 9

welcome to the War

with Ken Ham

> Be of sober spirit, be on the alert. Your adversary, the devil, prowls around like a roaring lion, seeking someone to devour. But resist him, firm in your faith (1 Pet. 5:8–9).

The family is under attack today like never before. Wise parents need to recognize this and develop their own strategy for protection and counter-attack. A generation is arising around us that knows not the things of God, allowing (and even encouraging) pre-marital sex, abortion, homosexuality, gay marriages, gay clergy, and easy divorce. By and large, they do not believe there is such a thing as absolute truth or absolute morality. Not only is this degenerate generation arising, it already *has* arisen. While a remnant of truth seekers remains, the attack on the family has the potential to eliminate Christian absolutes from our society.

The attack is coming from those who build their thinking on the anti-God beliefs that are destroying society. This attack on the Word of God has resulted in the demise of the family unit — the very unit God uses to transmit the knowledge of himself to each generation and the world around.

The central issue in the battle is what people believe about origins, for these beliefs determine their world view.

The attack on our kids is coming from several sources. Some of them are fairly obvious; others are right under your nose, and you probably don't even know it. Let there be no doubt that behind every attack is an enemy who is doing everything he can to covertly or overtly "steal, kill, and destroy" (John 10:10). Satan is using a barrage of tactics to try to bring down your child and your family. Three of the most destructive are 1) secular-humanism, 2) peer pressure, and 3) compromise.

Secular Humanism

"Secularism" is a philosophy that claims that there is no God — or that if there is a God, He is irrelevant. "Humanism" essentially says that in the absence of God, humans can and should act as gods by judging, choosing, and defining right and wrong for themselves. The philosophy pervading the public education system combines these two philosophies into one; one that teaches that there is no God, that there are no absolutes, and that anything pertaining to the Christian world view from the Word of God cannot be tolerated.

The foundation of secular humanism in our modern age is Darwinian evolution. That is why evolution and dating the earth to be millions of years old is pushed so much in public schools and other educational institutions today. Darwinian evolution and claiming that the earth is millions of years old are more than just issues of biology and age dating. At their very core is the philosophy that man, by himself, determines truth about origins and therefore life. Many don't understand this because they haven't been taught the difference between observational science (what one can observe and repeat — the science that built our modern technology) and historical science (beliefs about the past that cannot be directly observed or repeated).

Secular humanist philosophy has also infiltrated Christian institutions — those that have compromised God's Word with the world's teachings. They are training generations of students to believe the Bible is not infallible and therefore cannot be the absolute authority of God. The result should not be surprising, but it is still staggering: Barna research found that of the teenagers today who call themselves born-again Christians, only nine percent believe there is such a thing as absolute moral truth![1]

If you don't think the pressure is intentional or strategic, consider this quote from an American humanist:

> I am convinced that the battle for humankind's future must be waged and won in the public school classroom by teachers who correctly perceive their role as the proselytizers of a new faith: a religion of humanity that recognizes and respects the spark of what theologians call divinity in every human being. These teachers must embody the same selfless dedication as the most rabid fundamentalist preachers, for they will be ministers of another sort, utilizing a classroom instead of a pulpit to convey humanist values in whatever subject they teach, regardless of the educational level — preschool day care or large state university. The classroom must and will become an arena of conflict between the old and the new — the rotting corpse of Christianity, together with all its adjacent evils and misery, and the new faith of humanism.[2]

Whether in public schools, Christian schools, or home schools, parents must be aware of the influence teachers, textbooks, and other students have on their children. Non-Christian teachers without Christian convictions certainly cannot train their students in Christian truth. Because children under such teachers are trained with an anti-God and evolutionary framework, sinful temptations are often introduced through sex education, philosophy, and materialism. Because of their children's inherent tendencies toward evil and away from God, parents must be even more diligent at home to refute the influences of secular humanism.

Peer Pressure

Do not be misled: "Bad company corrupts good character" (1 Cor. 15:33; NIV).

I believe peer pressure is one of the most effective weapons Satan aims at your children.

It's a huge pressure on us as adults as well. The bad will influence the good more than the good will influence the bad: this is a scriptural principle and it makes obvious sense to anyone who understands the sinful tendencies of the fallen nature and the desires of the flesh.

Look at the example of Lot in Genesis 18 and 19. Did the evil in the city of Sodom influence Lot or did Lot influence Sodom for good? His sons-in-law didn't even believe him concerning God's warning that He was going to destroy the city! Even his wife looked back (longingly), contrary to God's clear instruction and was turned into a pillar of salt. Think about it — who really influenced whom?

Let's be honest. When in a pagan environment, do our children bring home swear words and "dirty" jokes or do the others take home the Bible verses? Which is more likely to occur? You know the answer — the former is much more likely to happen. This takes place on all levels, from individuals to entire nations. Remember what Jeremiah said to the people in Jeremiah 10:2:

This is what the LORD says: "Do not learn the ways of the nations" (NIV).

The Israelites were supposed to be influencing the nations, but instead they were constantly accepting the pagan ways of the nations around them, causing great problems and strife in their nation.

Over the years, we have sometimes been criticized as a family because we have been very cautious about who we let our children mix with. We have been as careful as we could be to choose the children and adults with whom our children associate.

Many years ago, a youth group leader in our church wanted our children to attend in order to be a good influence on the others (who didn't have the same sort of biblical standards we did). The problem was we didn't really want our children mixing with some of those others who might influence them for bad. We didn't think at that stage our children were mature enough to handle the situation, and so we had to make some tough decisions and limit our children's involvement in things that were even labeled "Christian."

Just because something is supposedly "Christian" doesn't mean it's safe. Many times desperate parents will send a wayward child into a Christian school, or to camp, or to youth group, hoping that they will get "fixed." Ignorant parents also send innocent, God-fearing kids into these same environments and forget about their responsibilities to protect and train their kids, thinking they will be "safe" because it's a "Christian" environment. The mix can be dangerous, as it is much easier for our children to be dragged down than for them to drag the others up.

Mally and I had to deal with "peer pressure" issues on many occasions, and we always tried to do it in a way that would set a good example for our children to learn, for their future role as parents.

For example, our daughter (when about 12 years old) came home and said she was invited to a birthday party and a sleepover at the home where the party was to be held. She said a number of other young people would also be at the party and sleepover.

My wife and I were immediately concerned about who else would be at this sleepover, and who would be supervising the event. In such an environment, we realized that peer pressure from others could have a negative effect on our children — and could lead to all sorts of problems, depending on who was present, etc. We knew that young people who didn't have the standards our family were used to could apply pressure to others to get involved in immoral activities, whether that be watching certain things on TV, viewing magazines, or certain immoral behaviors.

We told our daughter we needed to check things out carefully for her own protection. We called the family hosting the party and asked for more details about the event and the children who would be attending. We did not know this family well, but understood they were members of a church. We then called their pastor and explained the situation to him. The pastor did not divulge confidential information, but advised us to allow our daughter to go to the party, but certainly not to stay on for the sleepover. He had some serious reservations in regard to this.

Our daughter was told we would take her to the party and then pick her up at a particular time. I remember her being very disappointed. She tried to push us as parents to let her stay over — but we firmly and lovingly stood our ground. She went to the party and had an enjoyable time.

The next day, after she spoke to some of the others who stayed for the sleepover, she came and said to us, "I'm so glad I didn't stay for the sleepover. From what the others have told me, it was not good at all — it would not have been right for me to be there."

Lesson learned! And a child trained and protected as we believe should have happened in accord with our responsibilities before the Lord.

Remember also that children are not miniature adults. In this world of no absolutes, evolution, sex outside marriage, humanism, homosexual propaganda, and false religions — they will easily be tossed to and fro. They need to know how to recognize the difference between good and evil and choose the right way of thinking before being put under the pressure.

This creates a dilemma for those in charge of Christian schools, camps, and youth groups that involve non-Christians as well as Christians who have not been trained with a real biblical foundation. As a group, they seek to reach out to the lost, but the very people that they are trying to reach can put peer pressure on others to drag them down. This needs to be understood so systems can be put in place to deal with such a situation.

Compromise

We should expect attacks from the world,
but often the attacks come at us from those who
should be upholding the Word of God, but are not.

That's called *compromise*. Compromise produces people who do not see God's Word as infallible. After generations of compromised teaching, many in the church end up not building their thinking on God's Word, but form their world views on man's opinions. Many in the church don't understand the seriousness of this issue. Please understand this: *Allowing a man-centered system (fallible, sinful man determines truth about origins) unlocks a door for others to consciously or unconsciously use a man-centered approach to the Scriptures in all areas.* If man's ideas in biology, cosmology, and geology in relation to the past can be used to interpret Scripture, then it follows that man's ideas about *morality* can be used to interpret the Word of God in relation to the present. This is one of the reasons we see more and more churches agreeing with gay marriages, supporting the ordination of gay clergy, defending abortion, or agreeing with sex before marriage, etc.

It's distressing that attitudes toward these and other unbiblical positions have softened to such an extent that many Christians don't even seem to know what is right or wrong concerning such matters. How sad it is that some of the very things that destroy the basis of the family are being tolerated in many churches and Christian schools, and even parts of our Christian home-education movement.

Tolerance of man's beliefs concerning origins and the age of the earth undermines Scripture, and is in itself an intolerance of the authority of God's Word.

For example, the modern idea that the earth is millions of years old arose in the late 18th and early 19th centuries from the belief that the fossil layers had been laid down over a long period of time before man appeared. The fossil record is one of death (massive quantities of bones), disease (with evidence of cancer, brain tumors, abscesses, etc. in these bones), animals eating each other (with evidence of animal bones in the stomach contents of other animals), and thorns (supposedly 430 million years old). These beliefs are incompatible with the Bible's obvious teaching that death is an "enemy" (1 Cor. 15:26), that animals were vegetarian before sin (Gen. 1:30), and that thorns came after sin and the curse (Gen. 3:18).

Darwinian evolution also teaches that humans arose from ape-like ancestors. However, this is incompatible with the Bible's record that the first man was made from the dust and the first woman from his side.

Throughout the Scriptures we see God over and over again emphasizing the importance of accepting His Word as truth in passages such as Romans 3:4 which says, "Let God be found true, though every man be found a liar." To compromise the Bible's clear historical account in Genesis with man's beliefs about the past is to compromise the very foundation of biblical authority.

Many Christians don't realize that they, their church, and the Christian colleges they support really are compromising and are thus tolerating destructive doctrine. It is very important to understand that Darwinian evolution and the popular belief that the earth is millions of years old grew out of philosophical naturalism. (I refer you to the publication *The Great Turning Point*, by Dr. Terry Mortenson, for more information on this subject.)

Once the door to undermine biblical authority has been unlocked at the beginning (particularly in the Book of Genesis which is foundational to the rest of the Bible, to the gospel, and to all doctrine), it puts people on a slippery slide that can (and usually does) lead to a loss of biblical authority through the rest of the Bible.

This brings up another very important factor to consider. Which college do you choose for your children? Perhaps a compromising Christian college may be more destructive in some ways than a secular college where students can more easily discern the anti-God secular philosophies that they are being instructed in!

A California college student recently told me she was going to a secular community college, but her science professor was an ardent biblical creationist. Also, she had been brought up on creation resources and had a solid stand on the authority of the Word, and could defend her faith. She told me she had a friend whose parents sent her to an expensive Christian college. She said all her friend's professors at this Christian college believed in millions of years and evolutionary ideas — her friend was very confused and did not know what to believe about the Bible.

Even in "Christian" educational institutions, many do not accept God's Word in Genesis as literal truth. Most educators have been trained in the secular education system and often compromise truth without even really thinking about it. Many doubt and disbelieve much of Genesis — the 24 hour days of creation, the global flood of Noah, the creation of Adam from dust, etc. — not because of what the Bible clearly teaches, but because of the acceptance of man's fallible ideas about origins and the age of the earth and universe. A significant number of Christians, including many in leadership positions, compromise with evolutionary ideas/millions of years, and thus compromise with secular humanism as well — since secular humanism is a logical outworking of such a foundation in fallible man's ideas. Because of this compromising contamination, the culture is not being built up, but is decaying instead.

It doesn't take an architect or engineer to appreciate the necessity of providing strong and secure foundations under any structure. If the foundation is compromised, total collapse is inevitable. We can easily see the structure of society collapsing on every side (particularly in the once very Christianized West). The hapless politicians certainly don't provide any long-term solutions. Sadly, and to our shame, much of the Church at large is also bereft of comfort and encouragement. The solutions offered by many seminaries have their basis not in the foundation of Genesis but in the humanistic, anti-God philosophy of Darwin and the atheists. Their philosophies have so permeated most churches (and therefore our society) that they are no longer good for much of anything.

If the Church does not emphasize this foundational aspect (teaching God as the Creator and the Bible's account of origins as true and refuting the anti-God belief that everything can be explained without God), then non-Christians will not be challenged. As long as they don't have to accept Genesis as true history, then they won't accept God's Word as the absolute authority — and ultimately they won't have to accept *any* form of individual responsibility for their actions.

The compromise has actually trained generations in a philosophy like that of the Israelites in Judges 17:6. This was the result:

> In those days there was no king in Israel; every man did what was right in his own eyes.

This condition logically follows from teaching that allows man's fallible ideas to reinterpret the clear words in Genesis. When compromise occurs, man has authority over the Scripture instead of God's Word being the absolute authority over man. It's nothing more than humanism in "Christianized clothing."

This man-centered philosophy is not something that occurred overnight. Generation after generation in the Church was permeated with these compromised positions. After years of indoctrination, each subsequent generation tended to have a lower view of Scripture, even though many did not realize this was happening. Great men of God who clearly were saved, sadly (and in many cases unwittingly) contributed to this lower view of Scripture because of their compromise with the world's ideas. Such compromise did not affect the salvation of these leaders, but it did affect how the next generation approached Scripture — and the next — and the next — resulting in that slippery slide that undermines all biblical authority.

These compromises need to be condemned because they destroy a literal Genesis and the basis of the family unit (since it is in Genesis that the family is established). They also destroy the foundation of a complete Christian world view that integrates geology, biology, astronomy, anthropology, etc., because a true, scripturally based Christian world view depends on the history in Genesis.

God calls us to a higher standard in which compromise cannot be tolerated.

There is no such thing as neutrality, as Jesus makes clear in Matthew 12:30:

> He who is not with Me is against Me; and he who does not gather with Me scatters.

Scripture also makes it plain that if one is not walking in "light," then the only other option is "darkness" (see 1 John 1).

When secular schools in the United States eliminated creation, the Bible, and prayer from the classroom, they didn't eliminate religion; they eliminated Christianity and replaced it with the religion of naturalism. Such a religion is not "neutral," it is *anti-God*. Millions of students are being trained to believe that humanity can explain every aspect of reality without God — this is "darkness," not "light."

In Revelation 3:15–16, the Lord told the Laodicean church that He would rather they be either hot or cold. Christ gives them this solemn warning: "So because you are lukewarm, and neither hot nor cold, I will spit you out of My mouth." If we are "cold," we aren't affecting anyone; if we are "hot," and declaring biblical truth, then we are doing great things for the Lord. As soon as we compromise, we begin to cool, and then we begin to destroy; hence our Lord's stern rebuke.

As we train our children, we must take a stand for the Word of God and condemn error when necessary. This is something our father was an expert at! I recall the time my father received a daily devotional book from his church. He read the devotion on Genesis 6, and found that it claimed Noah's flood was just a local event. This made him very upset. He immediately sat down and wrote a letter to those responsible for the devotional and showed them clearly from the Scriptures that Noah's flood was a *global* event. He then went to the deacons at church and challenged them to stand up for the Scriptures and to rebuke those who wrote the material that undermined the authority of the Word of God.

On another occasion, a pastor told us that the miracle of the feeding of the 5,000 could be explained this way: *The little boy took out his loaves and fishes and thus set an example for the crowd, causing others to take their food and share with others.* I could feel the heat steaming out of my father while he sat in the pew. After the service, we immediately went up to the pastor and I watched my father show this church leader from the Bible that he had misled the congregation and had compromised the clear teaching of the Word of God.

On another occasion the same pastor was preaching again on the feeding of the 5,000 (maybe to get back at my father) and told the congregation there was a great contradiction in the Bible. In Matthew chapter 14 there is an account of the feeding of *5,000,* but in Matthew chapter 15 it states there were only *4,000.* I knew what was coming next! My father went up to the pastor once again and pointed at the Bible and then looked at the pastor saying, "Haven't you read the Scriptures? These are two different events! In Matthew 16: 9–10 Jesus stated, 'Do ye not yet understand, neither remember the five loaves of the five thousand, and how many baskets ye took up? Neither the seven loaves of the four thousand, and how many baskets ye took up?' " (KJV). The pastor had no answer!

What an impression this made upon me. It was all a part of preparing me for the ministry of Answers in Genesis, for later I confronted the same pastor about the origins issue. He responded immediately by saying there was no problem accepting evolution and adding it to the Bible. He told me a Christian could believe in evolution, as long as they believed God created. He went on to warn me about taking the Bible at face value, claiming that there are lots of problems with the text — thus, one certainly can't take Genesis as being literal.

As the pastor made these statements, I recalled the times my father had challenged him in regard to biblical authority. Seeing my father successfully defend the Christian faith against this pastor's compromised positions instilled in me the fact that I needed to trust my father's words rather than this pastor's and take a stand myself. Boy, was that pastor relieved when the Ham family moved on!

Isn't it interesting how certain matters become indelibly impressed on our minds — even from our childhood years? I believe that observing my father stand up for truth time and time again in my teenage years was essential to the journey that led me to what is now a worldwide ministry.

Yes, Mom and Dad, the war on the faith and the family continues, and there is no room for retreat.

> *When it comes to secular humanism, peer pressure, and compromise, things are either for Christ or against Him. There is no in-between.*

"Protect and Serve"

Many local police departments in the United States have adopted the motto *To Protect and Serve.* The sad thing is that most fathers are neither protecting nor serving their families, and have not obeyed the Scripture's command to be the spiritual head of the house. Fathers one day will stand before their Creator God and answer why they did not spend the time to ensure their family was built on the Word of God as it was meant to be.

Most parents have left the training of their children to churches, schools, or colleges. Many think that they can be absolved because they have spent much money sending their children to Christian institutions, but again, relegating responsibility is very unwise. More and more we see forces at work in our society that take our children at younger and younger ages to train them in anti-God philosophies. In effect, this is producing a non-God-fearing, anti-Christian nation.

Each of us should also ask ourselves whether we are among those who have compromised with the world, rejecting a literal Genesis, and thus helping to destroy the backbone of the nation — the Christian family. Each father needs to be obedient to the Scriptures and ensure that his children are trained in the truth of God's infallible Word. I'm reminded of what the great reformer Martin Luther had to say:

> Wherefore, see to it, that you cause your children first to be instructed in spiritual things, that you point them first to God, and, after that, to the world. But in these days, this order, sad to say, is inverted. . . . In my judgment there is no other outward offense that in the sight of God so heavily burdens the world, and deserves such heavy chastisement, as the neglect to educate children.[3]

Parents who are engaged and pro-active are highly important. I know this first hand. Beyond the sovereignty of God, the influence of my parents was the only thing that kept my faith alive during the years I was immersed in public education.

All of my "secular" elementary education was completed at schools where my father was the principal. In his day, there was almost complete freedom to promote Christian teaching. At the beginning of each day, the whole school would assemble. When we lined up and various announcements were given, my father made sure that we always started with a prayer. On entering the classroom, each class would have readings from the Bible. My father also employed discipline based upon biblical principles — and of course his Christian philosophy in every area pervaded his style of administration.

Because of my father's Christian character, he had a restraining influence on the whole school, which in the smaller rural areas affected the culture in the community, too. He applied God's principles in what he did as a school principal, and this permeated through the whole school, even though it was part of the secular education system.

Even under his leadership, students were really learning secular concepts in geography, history, science, etc. As committed as he was, my father did not have a fully developed Christian world view based on Genesis and the rest of the Bible as we do today. Later in life, as more and more creationist resources were published, he began to clearly understand this. Years later, I too began to understand how secular I was in my thinking in many areas.

I firmly believe that the influence of my parents and the restraining influence of my father's philosophy in elementary school greatly contributed to my spiritual survival. In regard to moral and spiritual matters, there is no doubt that many students, including myself, adhered to God's principles.

When I began high school in grade eight, however, it was a very different situation. There was no Christian philosophy permeating the school. The new textbooks were becoming blatantly evolutionary and clearly atheistic. I had to cope with an increasing number of students mocking me because I went to church. In many ways I began to struggle. I began to hear students talking about parties where they were involved in sexual promiscuity. Others would tell off-color jokes. The peer pressure was enormous. I spiritually survived, but only just. College was difficult as well, but because I lived at home, I really wasn't a part of the college environment. Still, there were a number of students who would attack my Christian stand on things.

My younger brothers will attest to the fact that when they went through public school (mostly after my father had retired due to ill health), there was no restraining influence as I had. They were also schooled in one of the bigger cities where things tended to be much less conservative than the more rural areas where I was brought up. (This is even true today in the United States or Australia — rural areas tend to be more conservative and sometimes there can be a good percentage of Christian teachers who can also have that restraining influence.)

My brother David tells of the immense struggles he had at school and how he succumbed to the peer pressure to be part of the crowd. What a blessing that years later he was able to put that behind him and rededicate his life to the Lord. Of course, such actions aren't without their consequences, and to this day there is much regret.

Matthew 7:13–14 talks about there being a broad way to destruction and a narrow way to eternal life with God:

> Enter through the narrow gate. For wide is the gate and broad is the road that leads to destruction, and many enter through it. But small is the gate and narrow the road that leads to life, and only a few find it (NIV).

I think most parents have a wrong understanding of this teaching. Many of us think of Christians being on one road that represents the narrow way, and that there's a *separate* road representing a broad way that non-Christians are moving on. As Paul makes clear in passages such as Philippians 2:15, ". . . you may become blameless and harmless, children of God without fault *in the midst* of a crooked and perverse generation, among whom you shine as lights in the world" (NKJV).

The point is that Christians live in the same world as the non-Christian. In reality, the narrow way is *within* the broad way going in the *opposite* direction. Most are on the broad way to destruction, sweeping along everyone else with them.

It takes a lot of work to drag our children in the opposite direction against the tide, because we have to work hard against the sin nature, the natural desires of the flesh, secular humanism, peer pressure, and compromise. How successful we are at this very much depends on how much we have saturated our children's souls with the truth of God's Word and modeled for them an authentic relationship with Christ.

Hitler proved that if someone could control the children for a generation that he would own the nation.

This should make fathers and mothers more diligent in ensuring that their children are trained totally in the Scriptures, recognizing it as the absolute authority in all matters of life and conduct.

The bottom line of course is that this is an ungodly world and there is no perfect situation in which to raise godly children. However, the more parents understand biblical principles and what constitutes a truly Christian world view, the more they will be able to discern the best things to be done in particular situations.

Parents, and particularly fathers, *must* be diligent in carrying out their God-commanded responsibility to train their children. There is no question about that. Foremost in the parent's mind must be that of creating an environment for sanctification that protects children from the immense pressures they face in the world. As you will see in the next chapter, that leads me to conclude that an excellent option for formal education takes place in the home, or at a carefully selected Christian school.

Key thoughts from this chapter:

1. Our children obtain their world views from their belief about origins. Some of the most destructive teaching in this area is right under our noses.

2. The teaching in our public school systems comes from an axiom of no absolutes and no ultimate truth. Teaching from this system has also infiltrated areas of the church, Christian school, and even home schooling materials.

3. Just because something is labeled "Christian" doesn't mean it is safe.

4. Biblical discernment needs to be first taught to children as far away from an environment of ungodly peer pressure as possible. They need to know how to recognize the difference between good and evil and act upon the right way of thinking before being put under the pressure.

5. Parents should never underestimate the damage that secular and humanistic teaching can have on our children despite the environment they are learning in.

Building blocks:

1. Be on the alert.

2. Engage and get involved.

3. Monitor carefully the environment and the material that is influencing your kids.

4. Don't assume that something "Christian" is safe.

5. Condemn compromise.

Questions to consider:

1. To what extent do you believe that Satan is behind the battles we face with secular humanism, peer pressure, and compromise? (Is that your opinion or can you back up your answer with Scripture?)

2. What areas do you need to immediately investigate to monitor the influences on your child? Where has his or her environment been compromised? Does anything need to be confronted to defend the authority of God's Word?

3. Are there areas of compromise in your personal beliefs and actions that are having an ungodly impact on your children?

Resources and tools:

Ham, Lisle, Hodge, et al., *The War of the World Views* (Green Forest, AR: Master Books, 2006).

Answers Academy, 13-session apologetics teaching kit includes DVDs, leader's guide, and workbooks, Answers in Genesis.

Terry Mortenson, *Millions of Years: Where Did the Idea Come From?* (Petersburg, KY: Answers in Genesis, 2005).

Terry Mortenson, *The Great Turning Point* (Green Forest, AR: Master Books, 2004).

Endnotes

1. Barna Research Online, "The Year's Most Intriguing Findings, from Barna Research Studies," December 12, 2000, www.barna.org/cgi-bin/PagePressRelease.asp?PressReleaseID=77&Reference=E&Key=moral%20truth.

2. John Dunphy, "A Religion for a New Age," *Humanist*, Jan.-Feb. 1983, p. 26

3. Martin Luther treatise, Letter to the Majors and Alderman of all the cities of Germany in behalf of Christian schools.

Autumn of 1966 — the Ham children at Sarina during the pre-Stephen years. From left to right: Robert, David, Beverley, Rosemary, and Kenneth.

CHAPTER 10

vegemite kids

with Ken Ham

One of the staples and delicacies of the Australian diet is a black paste called *vegemite*. Made from yeast extract and salt, vegemite is as standard in our diet as peanut butter is to the average American. Aussies like nothing better than to have vegemite on toast with breakfast. We call it "savory"; Americans call it "hideous." Most Americans, when given vegemite on toast, can't move fast enough to gulp down some water and get rid of what to them tastes horrible. Many compare it to chewing on bullion cubes; one person claimed it destroyed his taste buds for six months! Hey, I know the stuff is salty, but it's not that bad!

So why do Australians crave vegemite and Americans can't stand the taste of it? When I grew up in Australia, mothers fed vegemite to babies so they would learn to acquire a taste for this delicacy at a young age. Australians grew up loving vegemite for the rest of their long and happy lives.

Americans, however, don't get to taste vegemite until an Australian suggests they try it — usually as part of an ill-conceived prank. Because they have never acquired a taste for it, they can't stand it, and so will have nothing to do with it for the rest of their short and deprived lives.

What then can we learn from this concerning the spiritual training of our children? Is there an analogy? With just a little stretch, I believe there is. Just like children need to acquire a taste for vegemite at an early age, they need to be exposed to biblical input as well, so that they might acquire a craving for the things of God, and the sooner they get this input, the more they will desire the truth throughout their lives.

Sometimes parents hold back on spiritual training until they think the child is "old enough." That is a big mistake, and goes contrary to the biblical model. Think about these words written to Timothy from Paul in 2 Timothy 3:14–15:

> But as for you, continue in what you have learned and have become convinced of, because you know those from whom you learned it, and how **from infancy you have known the Holy Scriptures,** which are able to make you wise for salvation through faith in Christ Jesus (NIV; emphasis added).

It's never too soon to begin, and the more Scripture they are exposed to, the more they will absorb and become accustomed to the Word of God. As they learn to apply the truth that they are learning, they will develop the discernment to navigate through the temptations of the world, but this takes time and faithful feeding by the parents. Only as they mature will they be able to influence others in the same way. Consider this thought from Hebrews 5:14:

> But solid food is for the mature, who by constant use have trained themselves to distinguish good from evil (NIV).

When babies are born, they don't know about the Word of God. They don't know about Jesus dying on the Cross. They don't know what it means that God created in six days, and about marriage or any other Christian doctrine. When our first child, Nathan, was born, he didn't look up at me and say, "Hi, Dad! What are your views on eschatology and soteriology?" Without solid and continual feeding from the Word, all he would have would be the witness of a fallen creation (see Rom. 1:19–20), and an unrefined conscience alerting him to basic right and wrong (see Rom. 2:14–15). Our job as parents was to train him in that which is truth, so he could distinguish good from evil (Heb. 5:14), and not be tossed to and fro by every wind of doctrine.

> *Right from the time children are born, they need to be taught how to act and think as a Christian should.*

This means applying discipline in accord with biblical standards, having regular devotions and teaching times, practically applying Christian thinking in every area, making it clear that God's Word is central to the home, and protecting children from bad influences that they are not ready to handle. That's a given. We need "vegemite kids" of faith, who will eventually long for the real meat of truth, and then become salt and light to the world.

The Great Education Debate

What about when it's time to begin formal education? We know that parents have full control and complete responsibility for training their small children, but what about after that? What is a concerned and engaged Christian parent to do when it's time for school? Most families have three options: 1) public education, 2) private Christian schools, or 3) home schooling.

It is my contention that while children are still maturing, godly training cannot happen in a secular education system or a compromising Christian one. Personally, for our children, we chose a combination of home schooling and Christian schooling, with our last three children having been totally home schooled.

It is my firm conviction that in the majority of situations, home schooling is the better option, followed by carefully monitored Christian schools, followed by a secular public education. Mixed options may be available as well, as there are many Christian schools that provide infrastructure for home schoolers to attend part time. I know that there are exceptions to every rule, but they are just that, *exceptions*. I also know that circumstances may make the better choices impossible, but in general, according to the true ability and resources of the parents, I believe this order is best.

Home schooling has a long history in society and has existed to a greater or lesser degree in most cultures. In the last few decades, more and more families are choosing this option for their children. As the movement has grown, so have the support structures, materials, and curricula that are available. In most cities, parents can network together with other parents of like mind and values, sharing resources, expertise, and experiences — all of which can help keep costs down and improve the quality of the child's education. In the resource section of this chapter, we've included many sources of information regarding the option of home-based education.

Private Christian education is also an option. Solid, biblically based schools exist in many communities. The cost is sometimes prohibitive, and as we've warned earlier, just because they are labeled "Christian" doesn't mean that the faculty or the curriculum upholds the authority of God's Word to the highest standard, nor does it mean that your child won't be rubbing shoulders with students who will be a negative influence.

When it comes to public education, which is based in secular humanist philosophies, the Christian parent would be wise to heed the words of the great reformer, Martin Luther:

> I would advise no one to send his child where the Holy Scriptures are not supreme. Every institution that does not unceasingly pursue the study of God's Word becomes corrupt. Because of this we can see what kind of people they become in the universities and what they are like now. Nobody is to blame for this except the pope, the bishops, and the prelates, who are all charged with training young people. The universities only ought to turn out men who are experts in the Holy Scriptures, men who can become

bishops and priests, and stand in the front line against heretics, the devil, and all the world. But where do you find that? I greatly fear that the universities, unless they teach the Holy Scriptures diligently and impress them on the young students, are wide gates to hell.[1]

Some feel that the influences of a pagan education can be offset by being part of a strong church, but this isn't enough. It is a known fact that with each passing generation, greater percentages of teenagers brought up in the church abandon Christianity. Over 90 percent of students from church homes in the United States attend secular schools.[2] Barna research reported that 70 percent of these students plan on leaving the church after they finish school.[3] Those statistics should wake up any parent who desires to raise godly children in this ungodly world.

Both Steve and I attended public schools and a secular university. Looking back at it all, I realize that the only reason we survived the system was because of the phenomenally unique convictions of my parents, the circumstances our family went through, and the times we lived in — and of course the Sovereign God who was in control of all situations.

If a parent must choose a public education for their children, they must be all the more diligent to train their children to gain the maturity to discern right from wrong. The parents have to be even more careful monitoring materials and teacher attitudes. Perhaps most importantly, the Christian student must have a mentality that reflects the reality that they are going into enemy territory when they go to school. Secular humanism dominates, peer pressure is intense, and "compromise" isn't even an issue — the system is now blatantly anti-God and indoctrinated by Darwinian thinking that by and large won't even allow the things of God, or even the possibility of a Creator, to be mentioned. *The system is not their friend, and they must be aware and ready to defend themselves.*

Forming a support group with other committed Christian students can help immeasurably with this. In the United States, because of the "Equal Access Amendment," students can now legally form on-campus Bible

Clubs, prayer groups, and do limited group outreach. The restrictions on these groups can be significant, but it can be done. We've included more resources and information on the rights of Christian students in secular schools in the resource list.

Mature Christian teachers can also be missionaries in the pagan public system . . . and they need our prayers because it is becoming more difficult to be light and salt in such situations. Adults ministering *in* this system are very different than immature students being trained *by* the system. Until a student has the maturity to discern right and wrong, the strength to stand up to peer pressure, and the determination to confront compromise, public schools are a very dangerous place to be.

Keeping in mind that there could be restrictive legal issues in some countries, I stand by my recommendation that — as long as the parent has the ability and resources to do so — home-based education and carefully selected private Christian schools are the best options for educating vegemite kids — those who acquire and desire the things of God.

Oppositional Arguments

It may surprise you that the main opposition we get for the educational choices we chose for our children (Christian school/home school) doesn't usually come from non-Christians, but from Christians!

The Salt Argument

Often, the criticism we get sounds something like this: "Your kids should be in the public school to witness to the other kids; you need to throw your children out into the world so they will learn to survive; they need to be mixing with non-Christian kids so they can be an example to them," and many other similar arguments.

When asked for biblical references for such a position, I often get an answer that goes something like this: "The Bible says we are to be the salt of the earth. Our children therefore need to be in the public schools so they can be salt and light to the other students." Now, it is true that Matthew 5:13 says, "You are the salt of the earth," but let's look at this passage in full context:

You are the salt of the earth. **But if the salt loses its saltiness, how can it be made salty again? It is no longer good for anything, except to be thrown out and trampled by men** (NIV; emphasis added).

Mark 9:50 states something else about salt that is very important and must be taken into consideration:

Salt is good, but if it loses its saltiness, how can you make it salty again? **Have salt in yourselves**, and be at peace with each other (NIV; emphasis added).

The point is this:

A person can't be the salt of the earth until they have salt, and it needs to be uncontaminated salt that retains its saltiness.

Let's face it: Children are being contaminated as a result of their secular education, television, the books they read, and their friends. In a world of no absolutes, evolution, sex outside marriage, humanism, and false religions — children will be tossed to and fro. How do they know which way to go? How do they know what to choose? They *don't*, unless they've been trained in truth and can recognize the difference between good and evil in the world . . . and as I've already said, I feel very strongly that this training is best done in the sanctifying environment of a home-based education.

Because so many children from church homes have been trained by the government education system (which has become more and more anti-Christian over the years — to the point of eliminating Christianity totally), and because most fathers haven't really trained their children with a biblical foundation as they should, there are now generations of adults who attend church, but are so contaminated by the world that they think like the world. They lack salt, and the salt they have has lost its saltiness by contamination. These people then contaminate those around them and their own children. These children are often given no salt at all, or the little they have becomes even more contaminated than the parents' salt.

I believe that in many instances (not all, of course), what people call "teenage rebellious years" is due to a lack of being trained to acquire a taste for the things of the Lord in the early years. Once children become teenagers (and we all know that there are hormonal changes and certain behavior patterns related to puberty and adolescence), it is very difficult to change their behavior.

Contamination comes in many forms, but perhaps the saddest aspect is that much of institutional Christianity has compromised the Word of God, particularly concerning the doctrine of creation. Genesis (especially the first 11 chapters) is foundational to all Christian doctrine. Let me state my warning again: If generations are trained to disbelieve the Book of Genesis as literal history, and to embrace man's fallible ideas concerning evolution and an earth that is millions of years old, they are put on a slippery slide of unbelief through the rest of the Bible. If the Bible's *history* is not accurate, then why should the Bible's *morality* be accepted? After all, the morality is based in the history.

The literal understanding of the events in the Book of Genesis is necessary to an understanding of what Christian doctrine is all about. Sadly, some children from Christian homes are being contaminated by what are called "Christian" schools. More and more schools are being established on secular humanism and a secular curriculum, to which God is added, but you can't Christianize a secular philosophy! You can't have both!

If you are going to opt for a private Christian education for your kids, don't assume *anything* when it comes to the content of the courses or the convictions of the faculty. Don't assume that the students there are going to be a positive influence on your children. Do your research on the school; monitor everything carefully, and *never* shirk your responsibility to be the one who trains your kid.

No matter what education you choose, know that you must be pouring the "salt" into your children — and this salt should be as uncontaminated as possible. Children need to be taught to acquire a taste for biblical teaching as early and as repeatedly as possible.

This process is most assured in a home-based education where the parents can take hour-by-hour responsibility for the task. A private Christian education can also be a good option, as long as a parent doesn't forget their responsibility to monitor the environment and content of the education.

Yes, we are all called to be "salt" to the world. Our children are to be this as well, but they must first be filled with pure salt from God's Word — leading to spiritual maturity and stability, so that they can be missionaries to the world without being contaminated themselves and made useless for the gospel.

Good Kids

Some Christian parents justify their choice of public education by saying, "Yeah, but I've got *good* kids." Many child psychologists teach that children are basically "good" too, but the Bible teaches otherwise. Psalm 51:5 states, "Surely I was sinful at birth, sinful from the time my mother conceived me" (NIV). Scripture tells us that children are a precious "heritage of the Lord" (Ps. 127:3; NIV), and that they are a great blessing in a Christian home. Nevertheless, children, like adults, must be viewed first of all as sinful creatures, "For all have sinned and fall short of the glory of God" (Rom. 3:23).

I remember visiting the hospital in Australia where my sister had just had a baby. I looked at this beautiful infant and said, "What a beautiful looking sinful creature you have there!" (I was thinking of Jeremiah 17:9 that says, "The heart *is* deceitful above all *things*, and desperately wicked: who can know it?") I was nearly thrown out of the hospital, as you might imagine, but when they took this baby home, it didn't take the parents long to find out I was right!

Because of the sin nature inherent in all mankind, and the natural desires of our flesh to do evil, none of us should ever think that we are "good" enough to be able to resist temptation.

When placed in a compromising situation, we are more likely to be influenced by the bad than by the good. It's a challenge to get children to do what is right, but it is easy to let children do that which is wrong — just leave them to themselves, and they will express their true sinful tendencies.

Maturity comes with training, discipline, renewing the mind according to Scripture, and learning to walk in the power of the Holy Spirit rather than in the power of the flesh. That doesn't come naturally! It comes with maturity, and maturity takes time. Children are not miniature adults. They are unable to discriminate between good and evil. They don't have the discipline to choose between the truth and the cleverly crafted evolutionary philosophies.

Ephesians 4:14 states:

> Then we will no longer be infants, tossed back and forth by the waves, and blown here and there by every wind of teaching and by the cunning and craftiness of men in their deceitful scheming (NIV).

Paul also says in 1 Corinthians 13:11:

> When I was a child, I talked like a child, I thought like a child, I reasoned like a child. When I became a man, I put childish ways behind me (NIV).

The Bible makes it clear that children are easily led astray, easily tossed to and fro, easily deceived, and so on. Because of the sin nature and the flesh, a child in a pagan environment is likely to lose saltiness faster that gaining it, even if the parent is trying hard to fill the child with uncontaminated salt at home. (Consider how much time your children spend being trained in the pagan secular system compared to how much time they receive authoritative biblical input!)

When the child becomes a man or woman, exhibiting spiritual discernment and biblical maturity, then they can maintain their salt and be salt and light to the world. Let's face it, when we as adults are given choices, our sinful tendencies draw us in the wrong direction. Would you rather read the Bible or a secular magazine? Are you more inclined to spend time praying or watching television? Would you rather go to a missions program at church or a football game at the stadium? If you have some extra money, would you prefer to buy Christian books or a new piece of furniture or new car?

I'm sure we all get the point. It's not that we shouldn't read magazines or buy a new car, but we need to consider our priorities according to what the Bible says is important, and children who still have much maturing in the Christian faith are very unlikely to do this.

So, in a sense, what I'm saying is that the salt is more likely to pour out of the children rather than to be retained by them. One night, when our firstborn was in upper elementary school, he came and said, "Dad, someone at the Christian school told a dirty joke today and I can't get it out of my mind." Yes, contamination sticks with us — it is hard to get rid of because our flesh and fallen nature *attract* it. If we've allowed a lot of contamination to fill up these "vessels," it is going to be very hard to "decontaminate" them. That's why parents need to work so hard to avoid as much contamination as possible, and that's why dads and moms have to work with much prayer, patience, and perseverance to ensure as much salt as possible stays in the "vessel." There also needs to be much remedial work that reminds children over and over again of biblical truths that continually instill in them a Christian world view (and the more that happens, the more the culture as a whole will be influenced for good). These things are very difficult to do when the child is spending all day in an anti-God, Bible-denying, secular humanist enforcing environment.

Because of the fallen world we live in and the desires of our flesh and sinful nature, it is impossible to avoid all contamination. There are no perfect parents on this earth. We need to be aware of this and do our best to limit the contamination as best we are able, because our kids, as much as we might love them and adore them, are not "good."

Legalistic Concerns

Others object to my education recommendations by saying, "Wait a minute! Don't home schooling and Christian schools force Christianity down their throats?" Sadly, I have had people tell me from time to time that their parents harshly imposed Christianity on them, causing them to reject it. "I'm not going to force religion on my kids," they assert.

In every instance where I've talked to people who have been hurt like that, Christianity was imposed legalistically from the "top down," through pressure (and sometimes power trips) where the parent tried to make themselves the ultimate authority, rather than the Bible. When parents humbly start with the Word of God and build "from the foundation up," starting with the logical foundations of all the doctrine in Genesis, not trying to prove the Bible with science, but using the Bible to understand science, and teaching children how to defend the faith by giving them answers to skeptical questions of the age — then it makes a world of difference.

Christianity then is presented as a logical and defensible faith that makes sense of the world and is confirmed by real observational science, instead of what seems to be just a collection of opinions.

This is how we need to teach our children — from the time they are born until the time of our death.

Parents are to train children in the truth of Scripture, giving no options. For a Christian, it is not that truth is the *best* policy (as if it were one of several acceptable alternatives), truth is the *only* policy. Children who are merely *taught* can hear other teaching and easily depart from the truth because of their sinful flesh and their bias against God as expressed in their fallen nature. Thus, to cause children to be influenced for good, much work must be done. We must diligently *train* them in truth, condemning error for what it is. In Paul's letter to the Ephesians, he brings up another element that reduces the risk of legalism. Consider verse 4:15:

> But speaking the truth *in love*, we are to grow up in all aspects into Him, who is the head, even Christ.

In 1 Corinthians 13:4–7, Paul describes this "love" in detail:

Love is patient, love is kind . . . is not arrogant, does not act unbecomingly . . . is not provoked . . . bears all things, believes all things, hopes all things, endures all things.

I would propose to anyone who has legalistic concerns about home schooling, that when the truth is taught in an environment of this kind of love, kids will never feel like Christianity is being forced upon them. In fact, I believe the home is the *best* environment for children to experience this kind of love from the parent, even as they learn to fulfill the greatest commandment in all of Scripture, Deuteronomy 6:5–7:

You shall love the LORD your God with all your heart and with all your soul and with all your might. These words, which I am commanding you today shall be on your heart. You shall teach them diligently to your sons and shall talk of them when you sit in your house and when you walk by the way and when you lie down and when you rise up.

Even when home schooling or a private Christian education seem like the best options, however, circumstances can make it impossible. Allocating the time and finances for home schooling can be difficult for single-parent families. Many families depend on a dual income, and still don't have enough for tuition at a private Christian school. In other situations, there might be disagreement between parents when either the father or mother is not a Christian. It's also possible that a solid Christian school doesn't exist in your area, or maybe you live in a country like Australia where home schooling resources are very, very limited (or you live in a country where home schooling is illegal). These are all serious struggles, and reflect the fact that we certainly live in a fallen world where difficulty is a part of life.

If you are one of the people in this category, the fundamentals still apply. You may have to work harder than others and you may have to access more help, but you have the same responsibility to provide foundational scriptural instruction to your children. You have the responsibility to belong to a strong Bible-believing and teaching church, and you have the responsibility to manage the circles of influence that your children are exposed to. If you have no option but for your children to be educated in the secular system, then you must acknowledge that the responsibility of the position you hold has just been magnified, and therefore checking homework and monitoring your children's friendships will be of the utmost importance.

Always remember that it is your responsibility, within your means, to see that your child is trained and educated according to biblical principles.

God is a gracious God and forgives, but the consequences of your actions will still be part of the legacy you leave . . . and you only have one opportunity to leave it, so you better be sure you're doing it as you should. If God's people do not produce godly offspring, then the application of the truth of God's Word will be severely and negatively impacted for generations to come or to the world around. Who then will be our evangelists, pastors, missionaries, Christian teachers, and Sunday school teachers?

Key thoughts from this chapter:

1. We cannot expect our children to be salt and light until they first become salt and light. It is too easy to lose saltiness in an unsalty environment.

2. It is impossible to train children under a worldly system and then add God to it. You cannot Christianize a secular philosophy.

3. Our children are not "good." They have sinful natures and fleshly tendencies that make them highly vulnerable to temptation and compromise.

4. Building a defensible biblical foundation for our children allows them to develop a defensible faith. When done in love, this is completely different from forcing Christianity on them from the top down.

Building blocks:

1. The educational choices you make have great impact on the sanctification of your child. Make these choices wisely, according to biblical principles, and even at great personal sacrifice.

2. Always monitor the content of what your child is being taught, even in a Christian school or in home school curricula.

3. Never give up your responsibility to be the primary trainer of truth for your children.

4. Strive to always communicate the truth in love as described in 1 Corinthians 13.

Questions to consider:

1. In your community and church, what factors influence parents' educational choices for their children? Do you think these are valid? Why or why not?

2. Read carefully John 17:14–19. How can the principles in this passage, as well as the other passages presented in this chapter, be applied to your decisions about your children's education?

3. Consider three circumstances in which your child is exposed to secular humanism, peer pressure, or compromise. Is your child mature enough to defend himself or herself?

Resources and tools:

Websites:

www.gocampus.com. Student Venture. Find everything you need to be a missionary at a secular school.

www.aclj.org American Center for Law and Justice. To find out your rights as a Christian at a public school, click "On the Issues" and go to "Equal Access."

www.christianlaw.org is another source of legal advice in schooling issues.

www.thehomeschoolmagazine.com. is the website for The Old Schoolhouse magazine which is a good source of information on home schooling.

Books:

Starting a Campus Club (Gospel Publishing House) www.youth.ag.org, 1-800-641-4310.

Endnotes

1. Martin Luther, *To the Christian Nobility of the German Nation Concerning the Reform of the Christian Estate, 1520,* trans. Charles M. Jacobs, Rev. James Atkinson, The Christian in Society, I (James Atkinson, editor, *Luther's Works*, Vol. 44, 1966), p. 207.

2. Daniel J. Smithwick, *Teachers, Curriculum, Control: A "World" of Difference in Public and Private Schools* (Lexington, KY: Nehemiah Institute, Inc., 1999), p. 11.

3. Ibid.

Sarah and David, 10 and 8 — holiday
entertainment with shaving cream.

CHAPTER 11

submission, discipline, and nutrition

with Stephen Ham

We have an unquestioned responsibility to stand up and condemn error that is contrary to God's Word. This is very important in a world that has adopted a mindset that goes against truth and interferes with three additional aspects of building a legacy and raising godly children: *submission, discipline, and nutrition.* The biblical model for submission, discipline, and nutrition is our fundamental defense against the culture of this world. That is important, because the Christian family is also under attack by a crafty and powerful philosophy that has permeated the very fabric of our society.

The Post-modern Mind

There have been so many definitions for the term "post-modern." One of the common themes is *the abolition of absolutes*. Post-modern thinking does not really recognize one "truth." Truth is whatever the post-modern mind chooses to make it. *If it is right for you, it must be right. If it is not right for others, let them find their own truth without imposing yours on them*. That's the creed.

Tolerance is the buzz word that continually emerges out of post-modernism — and tolerance is a key theme taught to our children by the secular media, schools, colleges, peers, the community as a whole, and even in many Christian churches. Our society has embraced this concept of tolerance and has replaced absolute truth with an individual acceptance of what "feels right." In modern society, it is no longer acceptable to say something *is* "right" — now they say that it has to be "right *for me*." Adhering to the authority of one teaching (like the Bible), is seen as arrogant. I have certainly heard statements such as, "How can you be so pompous to think that you have the truth while I do not?"

> *The modern secular understanding of tolerance has not only replaced absolute truth, it has also replaced discipline and submission.*

The kind of tolerance that is embraced by the modern world is really *lawlessness*. Everyone does what is right in his or her own eyes. All through the Scriptures we see how this breaks down relationships. If we reject absolute authority, tolerance of lawlessness results. The family unit does not go unaffected by this.

In the suburb we live in in Brisbane, a large Islamic residency is taking place. New mosques and Islamic schools are being built and it is now a very regular occurrence to walk in any local shopping center alongside long-bearded Muslim men, as well as ladies wearing head and even face coverings. This migration of Muslims to our local area has given Trish and me the precise opportunity to teach our children about tolerance. To first do this, however, we needed to help our children understand some of the very different teachings of Islam and why the teachings cannot be tolerated.

We had to ensure they understood how the Qu'ran teaches that Christ did not die on the Cross. Fundamentally, our children needed to understand that if Christ did not deal with our sin in this way, we would have no hope of salvation, and by denying the death and resurrection and deity of Jesus, Muslims are sadly without hope. Tolerating the false teachings of a religion like Islam instead of teaching the truth of its error, does not help people to discern between the truth of God's Word that leads to salvation and the lies of false teaching that lead to eternal punishment. Tolerating people living in a cult religion does not mean accepting their false teaching. It does however mean tolerating them as people and loving and respecting them as fellow humans and neighbors so we can get the opportunity of telling them why it is impossible for us to tolerate their teaching and offering them the only truth that leads to salvation. This is true tolerance. We have consistently taught both Sarah and David that we are to love our Muslim neighbors not only in spite of their rejection of Christ but because of their rejection of Christ.

As we (with another family in our church) made friends and had picnics with a local Muslim family, our children have been able to see a genuine love and tolerance for our Muslim friends alongside a total intolerance of their belief in the Qu'ran and a true desire in tolerant love to help them understand the truth of Jesus. Our family has prayed together for these people, asking God to save them. This is the type of tolerance that needs to be extended by every Christian family but is very rarely returned.

In the realm of American talk shows, Phil Donahue dominated our television sets in the eighties and nineties. His show (and many others like it since) preached the core value of modern, secular tolerance (which is really moral relativism). The definition of tolerance on such programs is basically to *accept any behavior, lifestyle, or any philosophy, as long as it gives happiness to the owner, and as long as it is not harmful (however they define harmful) to the community.*

The talk shows that propagate the post-modern philosophy of "if it is right for you, do it," have not fully grasped the devastation this causes a community. Lawlessness is damaging to the collective individuals that cause it, those that act on it, and those that tolerate moral relativism.

The loss of absolute authority, coupled with an incorrect definition of tolerance, has brought about a culture whereby it is incorrect to impose truth on others and offensive to do so. This shouldn't surprise the Bible-believing Christian. Time and time again in the gospels we see that the message of Jesus was offensive to rejecting ears. When Jesus first sent the disciples out in Matthew 10, He warned them of such rejection and offense.

Mankind's tolerance of lawlessness has had devastating effects on culture and family. In Romans 1:18–32, Paul explains how "the wrath of God is revealed from heaven against all ungodliness and unrighteousness. . . ." As you read through this passage you will see the following themes:

- Though we know God, our hearts have been darkened, and we willingly live in lawless rebellion (1:21).

- We have put ourselves above God as the authority (1:22–23).

- We have exchanged God's glory for our own sinful lifestyles, and therefore God has given us over to this wickedness (1:24, 26, 28).

- One of the attributes of this authority rejecting wickedness is "disobedience to parents" (1:30).

Tolerance of wickedness is far from what God expects in the family unit. According to these passages, disobedience to parents is not only part of wickedness, but part of God's judgment as He gives the lawless over to wickedness.

Our children must understand the true definition of "tolerance." *Tolerance is only necessary where there is disagreement.* If we agree that someone else's behavior is not acceptable for us, but is right for them because it makes them happy, we are essentially agreeing with them. We are saying, "This is the right behavior for you. We agree with what you are doing." There is no need for tolerance where there is agreement.

Tolerance is much better defined where there is already intolerance. As Christians, we should be absolutely intolerant of the anti-God teachings of Islam, but our tolerance for Muslims as people should result in our love for them (based on the admonition from Scripture concerning our neighbor), and therefore our willingness to share the gospel with them so they can find true salvation in Jesus Christ. We should be absolutely intolerant of atheistic, evolutionist beliefs. At the same time, however, we need to be willing (out of loving tolerance for people indoctrinated in this anti-God philosophy of naturalism) to sincerely help those lost in this lie, so they can come to a knowledge of our Creator and Savior.

The fact that Paul explains that a child's disobedience is a product of wickedness and lawlessness means that it is obviously a parent's responsibility to train our children in the opposite direction to that of the lawless world.

> *This means our homes are to be environments of loving discipline, and God-honoring submission that lead our children toward a Holy God who is intolerant of sinful rebellion.*

It is normal for a Christian home to be opposed by the world for being intolerant of ungodly living and behavior. (Interesting, isn't it, that those with the post-modern mindset are tolerant of everything . . . *except* intolerance!) Yet we have no choice but to take a stand according to the Word of God. A Christian home is to be an environment for godly submission, discipline, and nurturing for the purpose of giving glory to the Almighty Creator. Our purpose as parents is to pursue these principles even in the face of the post-modernists' objections.

The Command with a Promise

In Deuteronomy, we read of the Ten Commandments that were given to Moses for the people of Israel. One of these commandments (5:16) stands out in a unique way:

> Honor your father and your mother, as the LORD your God has commanded you, so that you may live long and that it may go well with you in the land the LORD your God is giving you.

In Ephesians 6:1–4, Paul makes direct reference to this command, and mentions it as "the first command with a promise." God is ensuring that we not only know the command ("Honor your father and mother . . .") but that we also understand why it is important (". . . so that it may be well with you, and that you may live long on the earth.") This is a great picture of God's parenting. He gives *instruction with explanation* of logical reason.

In Deuteronomy 5 the people of Israel were moving into the Promised Land. They moved as one people consisting of many, many families. Living in harmony would require mutual respect, love, and honor as they were to submit to each other under the authority of God. These things had to emerge from the family unit. If they didn't, the nation would crumble. Can you imagine a community where parents honor God by being consistent godly parents? Can you imagine a community where children honor God by honoring parents? God promised that if they lived this way, their time in the Promised Land would be long and fulfilled.

The promise stated is the effect of a cause. Godliness displayed in submission and obedience brings about a blessed and fulfilled life in the Lord. In relation to us and this promise, Dr. Martyn Lloyd-Jones (the great expositional preacher of the 20th century) stated the following:

> Does that mean that if I am a dutiful son or daughter, I am of necessity going to live to great age? No, that does not follow. But the promise certainly means this, that if you want to live a blessed life, a full life under the benediction of God, observe this commandment. He may choose to keep you for a long time on this earth as an example and illustration. But however old you may be when you leave this world, you will know that you are under the blessing and good hand of God.[1]

A self-centered, individual-rights based approach to life is not taught in Scripture, and should never be taught or tolerated in our homes. A godly community is based on selfless submission and honor for everyone whom God loves and desires to be in His family. To this kind of family and community, God promises fulfillment and blessedness of enduring life, with a view to eternal reward in the Lord Jesus Christ. Adhering to this promise is what makes the Christian family salt and light in a selfish and unfulfilled world.

As we study these passages, it would be tempting to first focus on our children, emphasizing above all things *their* need to obey *us*. However, we would be both wise and humble to focus first on ourselves as parents by emphasizing *our* need to submit to our *Heavenly Father*. Each of these three aspects of training (submission, discipline, and nutrition) should be true in our own lives, that we might be authentic models to our children. So let's first look at our responsibilities as adults and as parents in regard to these three critical areas.

Parental Submission

Parents are a link in a great legacy of submission that actually begins with the relationship Jesus has with the Father. The family unit is to be a reflection of our Heavenly Father's relationship with His own Son, for we see honor acted out in the obedience of Jesus as He glorifies the Father in everything He says and does, even unto death on the Cross.

God commands our children to submit to us, but such a command to children places a massive responsibility on us as parents.

> *If children are asked to obey and honor parents in the Lord, as parents, we need to be giving them a godly example to honor and obey.*

This has been a very intimidating and life-changing concept for me; and it should be for you, too. How can we expect our children to listen and act under authority, if we are not listening and acting under God's authority?

Furthermore, we are not to submit to Christ for the sole purpose of being an example to our children. Our submission to God is to be absolutely sincere and genuine, an extension of our personal relationship with Him. We don't *pretend* to submit, or give the *appearance* of submission for the sake of our kids. We bend the knee to the sovereign and omnipotent God of the universe because it is the only right and appropriate thing to do. Sure, it will be beneficial for our children to observe our submission, but this is a *result* and not the primary *reason* for our heartfelt submission to Christ. We bow because He is the Creator, and we are the creature.

Christian Discipline

Accepting the discipline of God must be a reality in our own lives as parents; even as we desire to see our children accept our discipline. We are God's adult "children," and He has much to say to us about discipline. I'll let the Word of God speak for itself in Hebrews 12:5–11:

> And you have forgotten that word of encouragement that addresses you as sons: "My son, do not make light of the Lord's discipline, and do not lose heart when he rebukes you, because the Lord disciplines those he loves, and he punishes everyone he accepts as a son." Endure hardship as discipline; God is treating you as sons. For what son is not disciplined by his father? If you are not disciplined (and everyone undergoes discipline), then you are illegitimate children and not true sons. Moreover, we have all had human fathers who disciplined us and we respected them for it. How much more should we submit to the Father of our spirits and live! Our fathers disciplined us for a little while as they thought best; but God disciplines us for our good, that we may share in his holiness. No discipline seems pleasant at the time, but painful. Later on, however, it produces a harvest of righteousness and peace for those who have been trained by it (NIV).

That is as clear as it can be. God's chastening is a restraining influence, in order that we might conform to that which is good. As God chastens us, so earthly fathers are to discipline and train their own children. For this to be authentic discipline, parents need to "endure hardship as discipline." We never outgrow our position as His children!

While there could be many examples of discipline that I could share, (yes my children are definitely not perfect) in an attempt not to embarrass Sarah or Dave, I will let the precise descriptions pass. There is one thing, however, that I can safely share that will help you to understand something of the discipline process in the Ham family. I have never yet had a time when we have disciplined one of our children (even by spanking with a wooden spoon) where the hug and crying on a shoulder hasn't been immediately initiated by them. Every time this has happened it confirms to me that we are doing the right thing. The process is normally straightforward.

1. Take them aside privately and tell them that what they have done is wrong and that they will be disciplined.

2. Privately carry out discipline with self-control, explaining first to the child what will happen (e.g., how many smacks, etc.).

3. Hug the child and tell them that you love them.

4. Explain why the discipline had to happen and why their actions were wrong.

5. Talk WITH them about how they can correct this in the future and suggest alternative actions.

6. Always ensure understandings are God's expectations and not our own.

Every time this has happened in our home, step three has never been evaded by either child or parent. In fact, step three in the Ham discipline process has often been some of the more special times in our relationship with our children. It says that we love you unconditionally and that our children know that sincerely. When a child can tell you that they love you after they have received a spanking from you, it means they can sense your sincerity and self control.

I am not saying that as parents we have done this faultlessly every time. I certainly have made mistakes along the way (e.g., not admonishing in private or even allowing anger to rule instead of Christ) but even with a few sinful mistakes here and there, God has been gracious to us in the discipline of our much-loved children.

Adult Nutrition

To grow and be sustained as followers of Jesus Christ, 1 Peter 2:2 gives us this instruction:

Like newborn babies, long for the pure milk of the word, so that by it you may grow in respect to salvation.

Again we see the reality that we, too, are children — children of God; and like newborns, we are to continually be nurtured by the *pure* Word of God.

The Bible alone must be a regular focus of our diet.

Again, this is both a necessary reality for our own spiritual strength and a necessary model to our children. As we create an environment conducive to spiritual growth in the home, we should create our own environment for personal sanctification. As God's kids, we must make sure we are being fed the Word by others and passionately making Scripture the concerted focus of our own personal study and contemplation.

The importance of this cannot be over-emphasized. God's Word is sufficient, fully authoritative, and immensely powerful when it is accepted as our axiom and interpreted exegetically. We have already established that Scripture is the foundation of Christian parenting and the building of a godly legacy, but is the Bible established in our life as the sole source of instruction and truth? Do our priorities reflect this? In relation to our other interests, how much of our time do we give to focused Bible study? How does it compare, for example, to TV, sports, friends, and hobbies?

Turning to Our Children

With submission, discipline, and nutrition intact in our own lives, we are much better positioned to train our children in these same important areas of the Christian life. When it comes to godly submission and discipline, it is important to note that the responsibilities lie with both the child and the parent. Before we consider the specifics of a child's responsibility, one more parental essential must be considered: the command to train children in a way that won't exasperate them. Consider carefully Ephesians 6:1–4:

Children, obey your parents in the Lord for this is right. "Honor your father and mother" — which is the first commandment with a promise — "that it may go well with you and that you may enjoy long life on the earth." Fathers, do not exasperate your children; instead, bring them up in the training and instruction of the Lord (NIV).

Within this passage, Paul is directing fathers regarding discipline, but the message is true for fathers and mothers alike. As the God-ordained head of the home, fathers should take great responsibility for what Paul is saying, "Fathers, do not exasperate your children. . . ." Paul is telling us not to *confuse, abuse, aggravate,* or *isolate* our children and thus give them reason to disrespect or dishonor us.

No matter what we do, we should be asking ourselves if our actions or behavior could lead to long-term animosity in our children. This is very difficult in practice, and even while writing this book, I have learned a valuable and practical lesson. I have been guilty of disciplining our children without giving them any opportunity to express themselves or seeking to understand their point of view. Having a discerning wife who is willing to speak the truth to me in love has been an invaluable asset as I seek to lead our family. She has helped me to take the time to listen carefully to my children and greatly value whatever it is that they want to express to me, even in moments of discipline.

The last thing I want is for my children to grow up and say that they had a father who never listened, particularly when God's Word commands me to do otherwise. Galatians 5:22–23 describes the characteristics of one under the control of God:

> But the fruit of the Spirit is love, joy, peace, patience, kindness, goodness, faithfulness, gentleness, self-control.

A godly parent is a picture of the fruit of the Spirit. We are to be living in peace with God, and seeking His peace in our homes. We are to be long-suffering and patient in the instruction and discipline of our children. We are to be kind in every action . . . even in discipline. We are to be a picture of God's goodness to us. We are to be trustworthy and true to our word. We are to display gentleness with open arms and approachability. We are to be controlled and not given to temper, and certainly not to discipline out of temper or anger.

This is what Paul is saying when he is telling us not to exasperate our children. A life controlled in the Spirit does not discipline out of loss of control, but out of great control mixed with the other attributes listed as the fruit of the Spirit. Paul is not telling us in any way to be weak in our discipline, but to be reasonable. We are not to be unjust in anger or out of control in temper — because this is where discipline stops and abuse begins. Consistency and control is the key. We can be consistent and controlled by the Spirit, so that we can love in the same spirit in which we discipline — and discipline in the same spirit in which we teach and nurture.

In the context of Ephesians 5 and 6, where Paul is telling us to be Spirit-filled and controlled, we can have a great understanding of how not to exasperate our children. Ephesians 5:18 says, "Don't get drunk on wine, which leads to debauchery. Instead, be filled with the Spirit" (NIV). Paul is expressing the importance of not losing a Spirit-filled control. In the power of the Spirit, we can have a controlled and consistent life. This is a Spirit-filled life, the great key to understanding how a parent should train effectively so as not to exasperate their children.

Having established that godly submission, discipline, and nutrition begins with the parent who is led by the Spirit in each of these areas themselves, we are finally ready to consider training our children in each of these vital areas.

Submission: Children Are Commanded to Obey.

> Children, obey your parents in the Lord, for this is right (Eph. 6:1).

Children are required to listen and act under the authority of their parents. This submission, however, is not obedience under oppression (which is a restriction of freedom). It is also not a command simply to maintain the chain of authority.

Ephesians makes it clear that children are to obey "in the Lord, for this is right." This verse is directed to children; our children have a responsibility and they need to know what it means. God is giving them a command that they have the responsibility to implement.

The choice is the child's, and they are responsible to obey, but again, we need not make this more difficult than it has to be. No parent is perfect, but the more Christ-like the parent behaves, the fewer difficulties children will have in obeying. A parent who exasperates their child makes it more difficult for them to be willing to submit. Childhood obedience comes out of a great respect and love for a father and mother, and their obedience, like ours, is to reflect Christ and His obedience to the Father.

However, it is easy to look at this passage and start thinking about the impossible. How can we expect our children to be like Jesus in obedience? How can we train our children to imitate the obedience of our Savior God? Doesn't this place an unreachable standard on children?

Remember, God always calls us to the highest possible calling. For example, we are called to be "Holy, for I am Holy" (1 Pet. 1:16). While we live in this world, we will never attain perfect holiness in our life. However, we are called to live in such holiness, and we can only rely on the perfect Holy Spirit to assist us in this calling. In fact, the only way God sees us as holy while on earth is through our perfect substitute, Jesus Christ. Our children are called to be obedient in the Lord. With the assistance of our mighty God, we must help our children understand this calling in relation to Jesus and His life of honor to the Father.

As parents we should not, and cannot, expect our children to be perfect — but we can teach them carefully what their responsibility is to their Heavenly Father in relation to their earthly parents. Obedience to parents should be born out of a spirit of revering honor that is truly glorifying to God — and our children need to know this. Paul also says that obedience to parents is necessary because "it is *right*." Essentially he is saying that part of our God's righteousness displayed in our children comes visibly through obedience.

Discipline: Because Actions Have Consequences

When our first-born (Sarah) was about six months old, we were talking with my parents-in-law, Bill and Lyndell. I asked Bill (or "Pop," as I like to call him), "When should we start disciplining Sarah?" He gave me a great answer. Pop told me we were about six months too late in starting! Certainly, all discipline should be age appropriate, but he meant that we should take our responsibility of discipline seriously, so that our children can take on their responsibility of obedience and submission, and that we should begin right from the beginning. Bill is a great example to me as a loving and gentle Spirit-led father. Even though I am an in-law in the Forrest family, I find it a great privilege to join with my wife in submitting to Mum and Pop as great mentors in our life!

Discipline is an important factor in parenthood. It is impossible to teach your children the responsibility of godly honor and obedience without it. From the very first time disrespect, talking back, and general dishonor occur (and such behavior will, of course, occur), it is a parental duty to teach our children that such behaviors are not acceptable to us or God.

Parents have a great responsibility in carrying out discipline, and this should not be treated lightly.

Discipline is a tool of love that helps parents develop honor and respect in the household.

All of my brothers and sisters can definitely testify to the fact that our father's expectations in relation to respect and honor were very clearly defined. We were very clearly disciplined when we were out of line. While none of us were brimming with happiness to receive Dad's discipline, we would all testify that Dad loved us because he taught us well, even through discipline.

Some of you reading this book who know me well may be thinking back to my youth. You remember when my respect for Mum and Dad was almost thrown out the window. It was in those times that my father's discipline and teaching kicked in and impacted my life, reinforcing the teaching and discipline that I had consistently received my whole life. I love him, miss him, and regret the times I ever caused him strife — but I also know there is forgiveness from both him and my loving Jesus. Each of our kids must know this same love and forgiveness from us and from God as part of the process of godly discipline.

Corporal punishment is another biblical means of discipline that we are commanded to use — particularly as we understand the sin-nature of our children. Any parent knows that when a restraining influence is taken from children, it doesn't take long for them to start doing things which are not right, thus expressing their sinful natures. Most people have heard of the verse in Proverbs 13:24:

> He who spares the rod hates his son, but he who loves him is careful to discipline him (NIV).

In Proverbs 22:15 we read:

> Folly is bound up in the heart of a child, but the rod of discipline will drive it far from him (NIV).

Many other verses say similar things. Proverbs 29:15 states, "The rod of correction imparts wisdom, but a child left to himself disgraces his mother." (See also Prov. 13:24; 19:18; 29:17.) The Hebrew word for "rod" describes what we might call a cane, stick, switch, or paddle. When it's necessary to use the "rod," the child must not be physically injured or punished unjustly. The purpose of discipline is loving correction, not parental bullying.

My mother's parents lived up in North Queensland at the base of Mt. Bartle Frere. While visiting them each summer (winter in the Northern Hemisphere), our family would take a walk up to the pools where Mum used to swim . . . and each year my father would look for his new "cane" to use for the next school year. His favorite came from *Laywer* vine. He would cut several, testing them on his own hand. (His typical student discipline involved three swats of the stick, so he always tested them on himself first.) When he had cut several that he liked, we knew he was ready for school!

Dad was known as a strict disciplinarian, and even though he was never harsh or brutal, sometimes parents didn't care for it much. One time a mother became so mad at him for disciplining her son that she grabbed my father's shirt and ripped it off his back! One of the women who cleaned the school saw what was happening and chased the mother out of the school with a broom. And you thought that America was the only place with such antics!

Our father used corporal punishment at home as well as school. He always explained why I was getting disciplined, and I always appreciated that Dad would always tell us not only *what* we did wrong but *why* it was wrong. When we would get caught doing something, and we already knew *why* it was wrong, he would still tell us again anyway, just to reinforce the reason. We were never confused about discipline; Dad's explanations made it clear. (Yet for some children, discipline is confusing — and when they don't understand, it can easily lead to accusations of fatherly exasperation.) Dad's consistency and approach didn't cause me to want to reject him one little bit. On the contrary, I realized he loved me and was only doing what God had instructed so I would be trained for my future roles on this earth. I believe that most of the children who were disciplined by my Dad at school felt the same way.

Nutrition: Feeding on the Word of God

At the end of Ephesians 6:1–4, Paul tells us to "bring them up in the training and instruction of the Lord." This concept has already been dealt with at length in earlier chapters, but here we are again receiving a reminder that the teaching and instruction for our children does not come from us, a parenting manual, or a psychologist, *but from God and His Word*. I hope that this has soaked in throughout the pages of this book. The content and authority of the Word of God are indispensable components for building a godly legacy and raising godly children in an ungodly world.

The belief systems we have as parents have great influence on our children. These things show up not only in issues that are clearly biblical, but also in the standards that emerge from our own preferences and dislikes. As an old-school educator, my dad hated chewing gum, and told us horror stories about how evil it was. In our home, chewing gum was like the unforgivable sin. I know that in the United States, chewing gum is one of the four main food groups, but Ken won't touch the stuff, fearing that he will lose his inheritance, feeling as if he would be stomping on Dad's grave or something. Ken's kids are American enough to be able to chew without guilt, but my siblings won't touch the stuff.

Dad also found it hard to physically express emotion in the way of cuddling or kissing us as his children, and he usually addressed us with our formal names. I was "Steven," Ken was "Kenneth," but my father's consistent authoritative stand on the Word of God made up for any lack of ability to be an emotional person, and he displayed emotion in lots of other ways. I often saw him display great joy and deep compassion, and I even saw him cry once — in heartbreak because of a very bad mistake I made as a teenager. So while he did not often show his love physically, we all had no doubt as to his great and uncompromising affection for us. Even this has rubbed off on us. When Ken's staff at Answers in Genesis give him a hug, they say it's like "hugging a log!"

This is just to show that you, as a parent, have great influence on your children. The things you train them in will stay with them, making it all the more important to train them in the principles in the infallible Word of God.

From a human perspective, however, there is no guarantee that children will become "godly offspring" even if you are the most consistent Christian parents in the world. Each of us (our children included) has to ultimately answer for their own sin and make their own decisions to obey. Even though there are exceptions, as a general rule, the parents who don't train their children with a Christian world view reap the consequences in producing a generation who is not godly. As a general rule, the parents who do their best to train up a godly generation (even if not all are committed Christians) reap the rewards of such training, because the morals and examples of their parents, by and large, stay with them.

Deuteronomy 8:3 says that "Man shall not live by bread alone; but man lives by every word that proceeds from the mouth of the LORD" (NKJV). As we seek to give our children spiritual nourishment, we must again and again remember that true spiritual food comes only from "the pure milk of the Word" (1 Pet. 2:2).

Our Dad not only took it upon himself to teach us from the Word, but he also kept a close eye on others who were teaching us as well.

While my father would keep those teaching God's Word accountable to its authority, we would also see him overflowing with joy when God's Word was taught in truth with authority. When God's Word was compromised, however, he never hesitated to take necessary measures to protect us.

In my teenage years, the church I had attended most of my life obtained a new pastor and youth leadership. The youth leadership of the church consisted of fun, "cool" people whom I respected and looked up to. They were also teaching us to stand on our rights; telling us to not let our parents dictate our beliefs and values. (Post-modern thought was creeping in and causing increasing compromise.) A great chasm began forming between my father's teaching and that of the youth leaders I loved so much.

Unfortunately, while I knew in my mind and my heart that my dad was right, I chose to follow my youth leaders. This led me to actions that I have always regretted. Because of this, my father faced a hard decision. Should our family stay committed to the church where I was being led astray by false teaching, or should Dad find better mentors for his son? A pastor from another church (a man that my father and mother really respected) heard about what had happened and invited them to come to his church. As a result of my father's passion for me to be mentored correctly, and his passion for strong biblical exposition, we moved.

As you can imagine, I was really upset, but the result of this move had me sitting under some of the best teaching and mentoring I have ever received. My relationship with my dad changed as well. Instead of arguing with him about my right to believe what I wanted to, we would discuss what we had both learned from God's Word under the teaching of Pastor Norm.

Dad was passionate about every avenue of teaching I sat under. I'm eternally grateful for his relentless application of "nurturing and instruction of the Lord." Dad ensured that the spiritual food for his family was full of nutrition, enabling us to also understand the consequences from the junk food of false teaching. Many people today are choosing churches by the style of their music (sometimes mistakenly called "worship"), facilities, sporting programs, or some similar type of criterion. Trish and I have followed in the footsteps of my father to ensure that our children are sitting under consistent Bible-focused instruction in the Lord. We never forget, however, that the teaching starts by opening the Word of God in our own home.

A parent can and must do the things that Scripture commands. We are to be Spirit-filled, humble in submission, controlled in discipline, and faithful in receiving the nourishment of the Word. Beyond that, we must pray like there's no tomorrow! Because some day, as my father now fully knows, there will be "no tomorrow" — only an eternity that will reflect the way you allowed Christ to build a godly legacy through you.

Key thoughts from this chapter:

1. "Post-modernism" has abolished absolutes, resulting in a culture that values tolerance above truth.

2. Obeying and honoring parents promises a full and blessed life.

3. The essential commands of submission, discipline, and nutrition are part of a God-created plan that involves Christ's submission to the Father, our submission to Christ, and our children's submission to us.

4. Parents have the added responsibility to not exasperate their children and to be "Spirit-filled."

5. Corporal punishment is a God-given means of child discipline when applied with love and control.

Building blocks:

1. Submit fully to God in Christ. Make a definitive decision, before Him, to be committed to doing all that He commands in His Holy Word.

2. Review Hebrews 12:5–11 regarding accepting the discipline of God. Pray through this passage with God, asking Him to reveal its specific application in your circumstances, thanking Him for the provision of His Spirit that will lead you into truth and empower to obey.

3. Develop a flexible plan to receive long-term nourishment from the perfect Word of God.

4. Plan a special time with your spouse to discuss the principles in this chapter. Determine how you can best, as a team, fulfill the commands of Scripture to train, discipline, and nourish your children according to the Bible.

Questions to consider:

1. In what ways has post-modernism infiltrated your family, your church, and your personal beliefs?

2. Are you aware of situations where parents have exasperated their children? What attitudes and actions by the parents may have led to this situation?

3. What was your parents' attitude toward submission, discipline, and nourishment? How has this affected your thoughts toward the training of your children?

4. If you were to make one change to your approach to raising your children as a result of the principles in this chapter, what would that change be?

Endnotes

1. David Martyn Lloyd-Jones, *Life in the Spirit* (Edinburgh, UK: Banner of Truth, 1973), p. 246.

*Mum and Dad with Kenny and Mally and family in 1993,
standing in front of Mum and Dad's pergola. The Ham family
will very fondly remember the family barbecues had in this area.*

the family fortress

with Stephen Ham

In all the affairs and business of the family, even of the royal family, for king's houses are no longer safe than while God protects us. We must depend upon God's blessing and not our own contrivance.
— Matthew Henry[1]

Sometime in your life you have probably heard the statement, "A man's home is his castle." In Australia some years ago they made a hit comedy based on this saying, and called it *The Castle*. It's a popular movie, telling about a father defending his home and land from government takeover. The movie is filled with humorous insight into some of the lighter aspects of Australian culture, though a few sections of the movie are quite distasteful. The most impacting theme of the movie, however, is the relentless, one-minded focus of the father to protect his family at all costs.

My brother Ken and I have written this book with such fathers and mothers in mind. We have aimed our words at Christian parents who are willing to make every effort for the protection of their families. Our families *do* need to be protected. There is definitely a war taking place in society and there are two teams, God's and Satan's.

Satan is making every effort to persuade our children toward a worldly world view. He's doing this by attacking the very foundation of the Christian family: the authority of God's inspired Word. Ministries like Answers in Genesis clearly point out the battle lines and help Christian parents build godly family heritages. Throughout this book, we have repeatedly reflected on the sufficiency of Scripture, the authority of Scripture, the importance of a biblical axiom, and an exegetical approach to God's Word. A practical understanding of all of these concepts will help us defend our homes (and churches) from the attack and infiltration of Satan's worldly and anti-Christian influence.

As we begin to conclude, I would like to emphasize a biblical perspective that puts everything else we have discussed into a proper light. Certainly, we all desire to provide a home that is "a family fortress" against the attacks of evil, but in order to do so, we must recognize *who* actually does the building, lest we assume a responsibility that is not our own, or feel tempted to take glory and honor upon ourselves for something we didn't do.

Psalm 127:1–5 is written from a father to a son. In this passage, David is training his son Solomon, giving important insight to this very issue:

> Unless the LORD builds the house, They labor in vain who build it; Unless the LORD guards the city, the watchman keeps awake in vain. It is vain for you rise up early, To retire late, To eat the bread of painful labors; For He gives to his beloved even in

his sleep. Behold, children are a gift of the Lord, The fruit of the womb is a reward. Like arrows in the hand of a warrior, So are the children of one's youth. How blessed is the man whose quiver is full of them; They will not be ashamed when they speak with their enemies in the gate.

These five verses give us an essential perspective from which we can endeavor to experience a godly heritage in the safety of a God-protected family fortress.

Who's the Foreman?

That's a good question really: Who is the foreman of *your* home? Who is ultimately in charge of building the structure of your family? King David tells us that unless the Lord builds the house, those who build it labor in vain. This whole psalm contains great family insight and as we look closely at it we see important principles to guide us.

To teach us about the family unit, David uses the picture of a city under construction and the labor of those constructing it. In verse 1, we hear two clear warnings about the futility of labor without God. We can identify them because they both start with the word "unless." The first warning regards construction, and the second concerns protection: "*Unless* the Lord builds . . . *Unless* the Lord guards. . . ." These phrases certainly have special significance for Christian parents.

We are in the business of building our families, and we are also in the business of protecting our families.

But, *how* are we doing it; and *who* is really in charge of the building? David says that unless *God* is the builder and protector, we labor in vain. Psalm 33:16–18 echoes this truth:

The king is not saved by his great army; a warrior is not delivered by his great strength. The war horse is a vain hope for victory, and by its great might it cannot save. Behold, the eye of the LORD is on those who fear him, on those who hope in his steadfast love (RSV).

This is where the authority of Scripture and using the Bible as the foundation for building the right way of thinking comes into play in a practical way. It is a parent's responsibility to take God's Word as our axiom; the foundation upon which a godly legacy emerges. As parents, we confront compromise and uphold truth in order to defend our homes from the world's lies, *but unless God himself actually builds and protects, it will not happen. He is the One who in His sovereignty does it all.*

The building analogy that David uses is vivid. As Christian parents, we have the great blueprint (God's Word) to instruct us as we build the house (a godly legacy and spiritual heritage). As we build according to that plan, we look through our biblical glasses to be the watchman, staying awake, and always standing ready to defend our family's interest in godliness. In this way, we do not labor in vain, because it is with God ultimately at the head that the building is done, and in Him the protection is secure.

This principle is well documented throughout Scripture. For example, when a group of young believers began to divide themselves between Paul and Apollos, Paul chastised them with these words in 1 Corinthians 3:5–6:

> What then is Apollos? And what is Paul? Servants through whom you believed, even as the Lord gave opportunity to each one.
> I planted, Apollos watered, but God was causing the growth.

The apostle Paul recognized that it was God who gave him the opportunity to serve, and it was God who caused the results. We would do well to recognize this as well. That's the core message David is trying to get through to his son Solomon.

In fact, when using the analogy of "building the house," David may have been speaking directly to Solomon. How significant this message must have been to Solomon who was later to build the great temple for the children of God! Right from the first verse, David is imploring Solomon to *rely on God for everything, and to give all glory to God.* I wonder if Solomon pondered these words while building the great temple. We can hope so, yet how many times in history have we seen the greatest of buildings built as a monument to man, rather than God?! We only need to turn to Genesis 11:1–4 to find an account of such a travesty:

Now the whole earth had one language and few words. And as men migrated from the east, they found a plain in the land of Shinar and settled there. And they said to one another, "Come, let us make bricks, and burn them thoroughly." And they had brick for stone, and bitumen for mortar. Then they said, "Come, let us build ourselves a city and a tower with its top in the heavens, and let us make a name for ourselves, lest we be scattered abroad upon the face of the whole earth" (RSV).

The Tower of Babel was all about man glorifying man. People were filled with desires for their own greatness, intending to build their own kingdom. The tower would stand in honor of themselves; a great monument to human achievement. God's decisive response put a quick end to the blasphemy as we plainly read in Genesis 11:9:

Therefore its name was called Babel, because there the LORD confused the language of all the earth; and from there the LORD scattered them abroad over the face of all the earth (RSV).

This momentous event caused the separation of people groups across the entire globe. Through the confusion of language, God separated the human gene pool, resulting in the formation of new cultures. The very fact that the earth contains isolated and independent ethnic groups and cultures (whole people groups that on the surface look different to each other), should remind us of our sinful desire to reject God and glorify ourselves.

Today, we see an even more devastating consequence of this incident. The same human arrogance that was responsible for the Tower of Babel is now manifested in worldwide racial hatred. This hatred is plastered across our television sets on a constant basis. Every time we see it, it should be a reminder to us of what happens when we labor in vain without God as foreman on our construction endeavor.

"Safety is just danger out of place."

I have recently taken up jogging in an attempt to lose some weight and improve my fitness. When I jog with music, I tend to be able to run further. The words of songs can be very inspirational, and when turned up high, the music distracts me from the pain. (With the music blaring in my ears, it's a little tougher to hear the protests of my feet and the complaining of my lungs!) The music of one artist always results in a far better run — the funky southern-style jazz of Harry Connick Jr. While his music is not Christian, one of his songs always intrigues me. The lyrics describe how there really is no true safety in this world, and that "safety is just danger out of place."

We are responsible to do what we reasonably can to protect and build our home into an environment of sanctification, but in reality, there are too many factors, too many things out of our control for us to ever feel our family is "safe" due to our efforts. Rather than trust in God, those of us in Western society "labor in vain" to try to provide financial, social, and physical "safety" for our families. We strive to build successful careers, bigger businesses, and larger portfolios that we hope will give us safety and rest in retirement. As parents, we are tempted by society's values to create a better living standard for our family, desperately trying to ensure that our children are given every opportunity in life for their own future social and financial success.

Since the fall of Adam, everyone has faced the toil and pain of hard work. In fact, a life lived in disobedience to God (sin), ensures that we will have a life of toil and hard work followed by everlasting death (separation from God). There is *no* substance to life without God. He alone can give us the peace and life we work so hard to obtain, as Psalm 127:2 reminds us:

> It is in vain that you rise up early and go late to rest, eating the bread of anxious toil; for he gives to his beloved sleep (RSV).

Both David and Harry Connick Jr. are telling us that "safety is danger out of place." Yet David is telling us that there is no rest or safety outside of God. There is no way for a person outside of Christ to sleep well at night without the hope of a life in Christ. *Safety and rest for our family comes through God and God alone.*

When we went camping, our father used to classify people as either an "owl" or a "rooster." If we were making noise early in the morning, my father would say, "Shhhh! Don't make too much noise! The people next to us are night owls." Dad, as you might have already guessed, was definitely a rooster. He used to get up early in the morning and walk down the hallway of our home yelling, "Rise and shine! It's a beautiful day; don't sleep in and miss it!" Ken has inherited the same early-morning-rooster-crowing as my father. (Please pray for his family!)

Dad always challenged us to "make the most of our time" (Eph. 5:16), but what is the point of getting up early, working as hard as you can to be successful, coming home late, ignoring God as the foreman, and *never finding true safety or real rest?* It doesn't matter if you are a rooster or an owl. If God isn't building your home, you work in vain.

The sensible way to measure these things is to consider where God is in relation to your decision processes. Do you trust in *your* efforts and *your* resources, or are you resting in the *Lord* as your protector and provider? Are you teaching your children to rest in the Lord on every matter, or take the burdens of life upon themselves? If you are sending your children to a costly private school, is your desire to provide them with a God-centered and uncompromising Christian education, or do you hope it will lead to a successful and secure future secular vocation? If you are working overtime to pad your retirement account and expand your investment portfolio, are you neglecting the opportunity to mentor your children in the Scripture and thus godliness (which is the best "investment" in the future you could ever make!)? Are you striving to provide material things other families are buying for their children (things that will evaporate in time), or are you striving to build a spiritual legacy that will never end?

First Timothy 6 is one of my favorite sections in Scripture. In this chapter, Paul teaches Timothy how to deal with false doctrine concerning the desire for wealth. In 6:6, Paul says, "Godliness with contentment is great gain." What a simple and powerful equation! If a parent lives by godliness, and displays contentment to their family, they will show them what is truly important in this world. Contentment and godly living is infinitely more valuable than any material thing.

While the world talks about striving hard for material success, in Matthew 6:24–34, Jesus says something entirely different:

No one can serve two masters. . . . you cannot serve God and wealth. For this reason I say to you, do not be worried about your life. . . . is not life more than food, and the body more than clothing? . . . But seek first His kingdom and His righteousness, and all these things will be added to you. So do not worry about tomorrow, for tomorrow will care for itself.

In essence and in practice, Jesus says "I am your success. I am your life, I am all you need" (John 10:10, etc.). Because of our salvation in Jesus Christ, we are free from being measured by others in terms of wealth or position. No longer do we have to prove ourselves to prove our worth. *Our worth is thoroughly proven in the willingness of Jesus to die and rise again for our salvation.* The knowledge of salvation, and the love of God provide contentment, hope, and rest in our lives. That is something that the world can never understand or experience, no matter how much earthly wealth they have accumulated.

We sleep easy when our trust is in Jesus Christ alone. Anything else that we hope in for safety, is, in reality, a great illusion. If God is the builder and protector of our families, our toil is not in vain. With Him at the helm and His Word as our instruction, we will know peace and be able to focus on building an environment of sanctification according to His design.

The Blessings of "Billy Lids"

In Australia, we have an odd cultural phenomenon called "rhyming slang." We substitute a word with another word or phrase that rhymes with the original word, and understand it to mean the same thing as the original. Confused? Let me give you a few examples: The rhyming slang for the word "wife" is "trouble and strife." The rhyming slang for the word "road" is "frog and toad." The rhyming slang for the word "look" is "Captain Cook," and the rhyming slang for "kids" is "billy lids" (A "billy lid" is the cover of a can used for boiling water over a fire for making a cup of tea).

If I wanted to say, "My wife, children, and I are going to have a look at the road," using rhyming slang, I would say, "The trouble and strife, the billy lids, and I are going to take a Captain Cook at the frog and toad."

(The scary thing is that if you said this to most adults in Australia, they would know what you are saying!)

I have two billy lids, Sarah and David. If I give them a quick Captain Cook, as I travel down the frog and toad of life, I immediately see that they are a great blessing to me and my trouble and strife. (I'll let you translate!)

Here is my point: I love my kids, and it is impossible to describe what a great gift they are — a gift that I recognize is directly from God. At the climax of Psalm 127, Kind David starts with a big "Behold!" The previous verses have obviously been building toward his next statement:

> Children are a heritage from the LORD, The fruit of the womb is a reward (Ps. 127:3).

I am intimidated by these words actually. *Our children are our heritage, our reward. . . .* In this passage, God would have us place the importance of our children on a whole new level: They are part of His heritage *to* us. We are not just building a legacy *for* them; they are a direct gift *from* God *to* us. He owns them and has temporarily placed them in our stewardship, to build in Him, and protect from the evil world. What a responsibility! What an opportunity!

Children are a priceless gift, a reward from God to be cherished, and accepted with an awe of responsible stewardship — *because they are not ours but God's*. In the wonderful praise found in Psalm 113, the finishing verse exclaims:

> He gives the barren woman a home, making her the joyous mother of children, Praise the LORD!

Great praise is given to God when a child is born. The joy to the mother is like turning her from being homeless to having a home. In Psalm 127:3 however, David says even more. He tells us that children are not only a gift, but that they are a heritage from God. The word "heritage" has a broad meaning. First, it means inheritance in the sense of property or something you are given. Second, it means tradition in the sense of something that is handed down. Third, it can mean birthright or a given status.

Heritage

1. **Inheritance—something given**
2. **Tradition—handed down**
3. **Birth right—to live up to**
4. **FROM GOD**

The sense of awe in this concept comes not through the meaning of the actual word, but *where* the "heritage" comes from. We are not receiving an inheritance from a dead relative — nor are we giving some made up tradition or acquiring some worldly status. *Our heritage is from God.* We have been entrusted with an inheritance that is owned by Him. We are to build an ongoing heritage for our children based on His direction alone. If God hasn't given you enough sense of responsibility by acknowledging your ultimate reliance on Him in the building and protecting of your household, if you're not resting completely on Him for every aspect of contentment and rest, you're simply not breathing!

Have you considered the blessings of your "billy lids?" Why not do so right now? Stop your reading, do a little thinking, and thank God for the incredible gift he has loaned to you.

Now, "Fire at Will"

In the last two verses of Psalm 127 (verses 4–5), David turns defense into attack. Just listen to his language:

> Like arrows in the hand of a warrior, So are the children of one's youth. How blessed is the man whose quiver is full of them. They will not be ashamed when they speak with their enemies in the gate.

After reminding us that we must trust in the Lord explicitly for the protection of our family and for the building of our legacy, David tells us that children are weapons in the hands of a warrior. Obviously, any man with a full arsenal in his quiver (arrow holder) is a happy man. He is a man not disappointed and not ashamed in front of his enemies.

The wisdom and love of God is both a strong defense and a strong offense for the sake of the gospel in this world. In this way, a family is both a fortress and a lighthouse; both a refuge and place from which to attack, as it both defends God's Word and shines forth His enormous love.

At ages 11 and 9, through the grace of Jesus, my children grasped a sincere understanding of the gospel and received Christ into their lives. With strong defensive foundations in the authority and sufficiency of God's Word, Trish and I pray that Sarah and David will be lethal attack weapons (in a spiritual sense) for the sake of the gospel, bringing others to saving faith in our wonderful Lord Jesus Christ.

Our children have their own responsibility to trust and love the Savior. Nonetheless, our own home is our first mission field, the place we are to equip them to be able take up this responsibility of one day reaching out to the world themselves. Our children are born sinful, and we have the opportunity to introduce them to the saving power of Jesus Christ and then train them as missionaries to reach their own future families and the world.

I pray that you fully consider the significance of these passages and *all* passages in Scripture. Since Psalm 127 was written by David to Solomon, perhaps we should give David's son the last say in regard to this matter. In Proverbs 27:11 Solomon says to his own son:

> Be wise, my son, and make my heart glad, That I may reply to him who reproaches me.

Solomon understood the teaching of his own father in this statement. If you read through Proverbs, you will find that many of them start with Solomon saying to his son, "Listen to me," or "My son, be attentive to wisdom." As part of this legacy, parents therefore need to uphold the absolute authority of God's Word, and a consistent biblical foundation.

PARENTS ARE PEOPLE WHO:

1. **RELY ON GOD FOR BUILDING AND PROTECTION**

2. **ARE WARNED ABOUT DISTRACTION**

3. **ARE GRATEFUL IN THEIR CALLING**

4. **ARE COMMITTED TO THE COMMISSION**

We need to submit, rely, trust, and give all family matters over to God and the authority of His Word.

It is impossible to do this as consistent godly parents if we make worldly pursuits our priority, and make worldly post-modern wisdom our authority by accepting compromise and tolerating ungodly teaching. We can't build our own house on the lies of Satan and then hope that God will protect the heritage that He entrusted us with.

Unless God builds your house, you labor in vain.

God demands parental allegiance, and that allegiance begins and ends with a clear mandate: *The raising of godly children in an ungodly world begins and ends with the content and the authority of God and His Word.* He is the foreman of what we desire to build, He is the owner of all we have, and we never cease to be His children — not even as we seek to raise the children He has temporarily entrusted to us.

One Last Important Point
With Ken Ham

I hope the words of this chapter and this book have touched your heart and stirred your conscience. There is no doubt that being a parent in the modern world is a demanding and all-consuming task. Our desire is that God will somehow use these principles of Scripture and challenge you to build a godly legacy in His name for the sake of your children, your community, and our world.

Certainly, there is much to be done as parents. The principles from God's Holy Word have shown us the foundation, components, and process for building a godly legacy. God commands and expects that we will take responsibility for the things that He has called us to take action on, and then to trust Him with all the results. Yet Steve and I carry with us a concern as well. We fear that in sharing our story and giving tribute to our father and mother, that we would somehow attract glory toward ourselves or our parents, or take credit for what He has done . . . something that our father would be appalled by.

We are more amazed than anyone about the way that God has chosen to use us as He has. He has done so in spite of our sin, our weaknesses, our fallen hearts, and our flesh. That's why we wanted to close with this chapter on building a "family fortress." Our desire is that the words of David from Psalm 127:1 will be continually at the forefront of your mind:

> *Unless the Lord* builds the house . . .
> *Unless the Lord* guards the city. . . .

If we think that our efforts are ultimately responsible for the type of legacy we are leaving, we set ourselves up for one of two certain errors: 1) We will either feel guilt and failure when things go "bad," or 2) we will feel pride and arrogance when things turn out "well." It's your responsibility to be faithful to the principles of God's Word, but *unless the Lord* builds and watches, it will all be for naught. We *are* called to action and belief, but we are entirely dependent on Him for the outcome. He alone can change hearts; He alone can design the heritage; He alone can build the legacy in a way that brings glory to His name.

That leads me to one last challenge of Scripture: The challenge to be parents of prayer. Heartfelt prayer expresses our dependence upon God to "build the house." Earnest prayer praises God for His attributes and acknowledges Him as the Creator and sustainer of all things. Obedient prayer is a response to the perfect and authoritative Word of God which calls us to pray. Regular prayer is a privilege, allowing us to have focused intimacy with Him and give thanks to Him as our perfect provider of all things.

If you were to ask me what stands out in regard to my mother, I would have to say that Mum is a valiant and beautiful woman of prayer. One of my earliest memories in life is of my mother tucking me into bed, holding my hands together, and teaching me to pray. Each night she would close our time with the Lord with the same, simple recited prayer. She hasn't said this prayer with me for many decades, but it has been etched in my mind forever:

> Jesus tender shepherd hear me,
> Bless thy little lamb tonight,
> Through the darkness be thou near me,
> Watch my sleep till morning light.
> May all my sins be all forgiven,
> Bless the friends I love so well,
> Take me when I die to heaven,
> There with thee to dwell.

The fact that I can remember this prayer at all tells me something about our mother. She understood from God's Word the importance of prayer, and she acted on that understanding. Matthew 6:6 states:

> But you, when you pray, go into your room, and when you have shut your door, pray to your Father who is in the secret place; and your Father who sees in secret will reward you openly (NKJV).

Jesus didn't say "if" you pray, He said "when"! Prayer is not an option! It is a command that we see over and over in the Bible. It is certainly something our mother understood as she and Dad trained up their children in the ways of the Lord.

Our mother would tell us often that she was praying for us. After we left home and started our own families, Mum would often say, "I pray for you every day." Sometimes she would tell me she had been praying all night about a particular situation. First Thessalonians 5:17 commands us to "pray without ceasing." When I think of this verse, I think of Mum.

She has always been a great prayer warrior. Of course, this has also had a great effect on Mally and me, and is reflected in how we brought up our own children. Not only did my wife and I spend time praying that the Lord might allow us to have children to train for Him (and He granted that request with all five of them), but we prayed for our children in the womb, we prayed for them when they were born, and we continue to pray for them daily . . . just like Mum.

We need to certainly build all our thinking in regard to raising our children on the Word of God — but no matter how diligent we are in applying the principles from God's Word, we still need to "pray without ceasing" for our children. We need to teach them to pray . . . not meaningless prayers of repeated words, but prayers that reflect the living truth of God's Word and the deepest desires and passions of our hearts.

I remember an incident when we still lived in Australia that illustrates the importance of our children seeing us pray and learning to pray themselves. Nathan and Renee (our two oldest children) were only around five and six years old. They were outside playing, when they suddenly came running into the house creating alarm. Renee had accidently dropped a brick on Nathan's thumb. When he held up his bleeding thumb, it looked like a mangled piece of flesh. I'll never forget what happened next:

Renee said, "We need to pray! We need to ask Jesus to fix Nathan's thumb." After a few days, his thumb did heal, without any permanent damage — and of course we thanked the Lord that Nathan's thumb returned to normal. The incident reminds us not only of God's willingness to heal, but of the need for us to have the mustard seed-like faith of a child in all our prayers.

When you look at a ministry like Answers in Genesis and the giant steps of faith we have taken over the years, it should also be understood that there has been much prayer behind all this. Not only have my wife and I prayed much — but our children, also. Of course, Dad and Mum must have spent countless hours praying for us — and praying for the ministries all of the Ham siblings have been involved in.

I send my mother my itinerary and she prays for me as I travel and for all the speaking engagements I'm involved in. She tells me that every time I fly, she prays for the plane the whole way until she knows I've safely arrived at my destination. Sometimes when I board a plane, I think I should get on the public address system and say, "Relax, people. You are all being prayed for by a great prayer warrior as we fly today!" I smile to myself and think, *These people don't know it, but my mum is really praying for them!* Prayer is essential for our journey as parents as well, that we might reach our goal to create a legacy by raising godly children in this ungodly world.

A book of this type — concerning the training of children in the Lord — would not be complete without a challenge concerning a matter so vital as prayer. Prayer must be brought to our attention, lest we neglect it. The unchanging truth of God's Word is our inerrant foundation. Heart-felt conviction, a vibrant personal relationship with Christ, and an understanding of our roles and responsibilities are the components with which we build. In the end, unless God builds the house, we labor in vain. Prayer is a genuine response to these principles, and an authentic communication of praise, thanksgiving, and petition.

May God himself draw us to our knees as we desire to take a stand for Him and His Holy Word.

Key thoughts from this chapter:

1. Our children are not a monument to ourselves. To raise them apart from God's guidance and truth is a direct rejection of God's authority.

2. There is no rest or safety outside of God. Excessive toiling for things that do not provide an eternal benefit is ultimately of no benefit at all.

3. Our children are given to us *from* God and *for* God. If we take this seriously, it is an intimidating and exciting opportunity.

4. According to Psalm 127, our children are to become servants of the gospel for the ultimate honor and glory of God and extension of His kingdom.

Building blocks:

1. Contemplate Psalm 139:23–24 and ask God to search your heart and reveal your ways. As He shows you areas where you are trusting in your own toil, rather than on Him, for creating an environment for sanctification and a family fortress, commit those areas to Him, confessing that He alone can build and protect.

2. Communicate to your children, in any way you wish, that you see them as a blessing from God, for God.

3. Jesus gave specific instructions on "how to pray" in Matthew 6:5–14. Carefully review this passage, noting both specific guidelines and general principles that Christ gave regarding it.

4. Using these principles, make a flexible plan for special times of prayer.

Questions to consider:

1. In the region where you live, do you see examples of people who are driven to excessive toil in search of safety? What is the result of this?

2. How will you know when your children are arrows who are "ready to fire" into the world for God? Are there steps you can be taking now to train them for this purpose?

3. A biblical world view is not complete without a clear understanding of who we are and who protects our families and builds our home. What do the following verses say about this important topic? What is the result of a life that is lived according to these principles of infallible truth?

> John 15:4–5
> Philippians 4:10–13
> 1 Timothy 6:14–16

Endnotes

1. Matthew Henry, *A Commentary on the Whole Bible*, Vol. 3, p. 734, www.ccel.org/h/henry/mhc2/MHC00000.HTM.

Dad, doing a devotion for an American tour group in 1992 at Paul and Rosemary's house in Brisbane.

the revelation of a legacy

with Ken Ham

Sometimes, a single phone call can change your whole life . . . and change it forever. In June of 1995, we all knew "the call" was coming, and prepared ourselves as best we could. In many ways we had had a lifetime to prepare for it as we observed Mum and Dad walk with God in light of eternity, but this felt different, for now Dad was preparing to take the final step. He had been sick off and on for some time, and this time we knew that he would not be getting better.

Still, as ready as we were, and as ready as Dad was, the phone calls still seemed to stop the rotation of earth, dislodging everything that seemed immovable. Steve remembers it this way:

I was living in Clermont, a small country town in North Queensland, approximately 12 hours' drive from Mum and Dad in Brisbane. The call came in the early hours of the morning. It was my brother Rob. He said it was time to come home; Dad might not have long to live. Things that seemed so important and urgent only a few hours before were dropped and forgotten. We quickly threw some essentials in the car and began a desperate dash across the Australian plains and down the coast. Odd, but even after a lifetime together, there was so much I wanted to say . . . so many things to tell him "thank you" for. As the road and the hours slipped away, I hoped (for my sake) that he would stay a little longer. I wanted to see him one last time before his "promotion to glory"; but more importantly, I wanted to hug my dad goodbye.

As we sped through the day, I thought of my father's attributes and his ways. There was much to contemplate, but two things kept coming back to mind: his commitment to God's Word, and his challenge to me to be a man of that Word. A few weeks earlier he and Mum had visited us in Clermont and presented me with a copy of *Willmington's Guide to the Bible*. Inscribed in the front cover was the last piece of writing I would ever receive from my father:

> To Stephen and Trish,
> with love from Mum and Dad.
> Be diligent to present yourself approved to God as a
> workman who does not need to be ashamed, handling
> accurately the Word of Truth (2 Timothy 2:15).

We arrived in Brisbane in record-breaking time. Dad had stabilized somewhat, and it would turn out that I would have one whole week with my father. Together with my other brothers and sisters, we laughed and cried and prayed; talking about so many blessings, remembering so many things from the years past. During this blessed week I was able to hear my father telling me of his confidence in the eternal glory, and his pleasure in the Lord in his life on earth. The days drifted by as we all waited for the time that the Lord would lovingly take my father into the gates of heaven. There was, however, a notable absence. Kenny was not with us, and because of the bond that our family has together in the Lord Jesus, we all desperately felt this absence.

In the few hours before that appointed moment, I had the opportunity to talk to Dad just one more time. In the waiting room, with the rest of the family taking turns with him, I awaited with uncertainty to have my last conversation with Dad. It wasn't that I didn't know what I wanted to say to him — because I knew that exactly — more concerning to me was whether I would be able to get the words out beyond the massive lump that had suddenly formed in my throat.

My turn came, and I looked at my brothers and sisters with a feeling of despair, and went into Dad's room. Mum was at his side weeping and kissing his hand. I looked in his eyes, choked back the tears and said "*Dad, I want to promise you that I will try my best to be a godly leader in my family and bring up my children for the Lord the same way you did for us.*" With his oxygen mask on he had no way to give me a clear verbal response, but the joy on his face will be burned into my memory for the rest of my days — and every time I remember it, I will remember my promise not only to him, but to God. I gave him that hug, kissed him on his forehead, and left the room, returning to the loving embrace and tears of my brothers and sisters in the waiting room.

A short time later, Dad entered eternity and embraced the One whom he had believed, loved, and served by faith.

As Steve and my siblings in Australia escorted Dad to the threshold of eternal life, I was sitting in a hotel room in Indianapolis, Indiana. The call came on the 9th of June. It was my brother Robert. The news grabbed my heart and I sank onto the bed, doing my best just to breathe. So many things were flashing through my mind, but it was like being in a daze.

Nothing connected. In my room and outside my window, everything appeared to be the same, but with that one brief phone call, everything was different.

The phone rang once more — it was the local Christian radio station calling for an interview to promote the seminar I was speaking at. I answered the questions and tried to act as my normal self, but nothing felt normal. As if on autopilot, I picked up my briefcase and walked across the road and parking lot to the Indianapolis Convention Center. It seemed like such a long walk, almost as if time had stopped completely. I took a deep breath, entered the auditorium, took my place at the podium in front of hundreds of people, and somehow began my lecture. . . .

Dad and I had talked many times over the years as to what I should do if he were to die while I was conducting a seminar. Knowing my father was seriously ill, I could have cancelled the seminar and traveled home (36 hours usually, including around 20 hours of flying). Dad had told me on more than one occasion that he had trained us to love God's Word and there was nothing more important than to tell people about Christ. He said, "Kenneth, if I die there's really no point in coming back, because I won't be here. It will be more important to preach God's Word so others can join me in heaven."

So I had decided to stay and speak at the seminar — this is what my father would want and I wanted to honor his request. By the grace of God, I was able to complete my messages that day and over the next several days.

Meanwhile, a burial service for family and close friends was conducted at the cemetery a few miles from our family home. A close friend video-taped the service so I could view it later. When the seminars were complete, Mally and I boarded a plane with our children and flew to Australia for a special memorial service for Dad on the 25th of June. It was an emotional homecoming, as I embraced Mum and faced my father's physical absence for the first time. I had come home to give honor to my dad, but it turned out that he had one last earthly gift for me.

In the months before Dad died, he had constructed a model of Noah's ark. True to the dimensions in Scripture, he had built the small craft to scale and weighted it properly so that it could withstand waves without turning over. My father wasn't a carpenter, but he put his heart and soul into making this model something special. When I arrived home, it was there, floating in the pool, flying miniature flags from both Australia and the United States.

The ark my father built for me rests with pride on the bookshelf in my office at Answers in Genesis. Each time I look at it I am reminded of the inheritance my parents gave me — an inheritance that is far more valuable than silver or gold. They left an everlasting spiritual inheritance: a love for the Creator and Savior and His infallible Word.

At the memorial service, my five brothers and sisters and I shared our testimonies concerning Dad. We all used different terminology and phraseology — but our words conveyed the same basic theme:

Dad never knowingly wanted to compromise the Word of God.

Dad always stood up for what he believed.

Dad taught his children to love the Word of God.

Dad always wanted God's Word to be in authority over the fallible words of man.

Dad hated compromise and would actively contend for the Christian faith.

Dad understood the foundational importance of the inerrant, infallible, inspired Word of God.

This was what we shared about our Dad. At the end of the service, a dear friend of the family came up to me and said, "After a service like that, I'm challenged to go home and ask my children what they're going to say about me when I'm dead!" His question sparked Steve's and my vision for this book, knowing that the question is one that all who desire to raise godly children in this ungodly world should ask. *What will your children say about you when you die?*

During the service, Steve shared a poem that sums up our family's feelings, encapsulating the thoughts of all of us six kids:

A Jesus Focused Life

The immense and wondrous glory of our mighty sovereign God,
Is much too great for us to understand.
He is perfect in His power, He's present everywhere,
He knows the number of each grain of sand.

And yet sometimes we act as if our Lord does not exist,
We live as if we're living all alone.
So let me tell you of a man who lived to glorify his Maker,
And took the gospel truth to be his own.

Dad searched for opportunities to talk about his Savior,
His focus was on Jesus to the end.
He strove to glorify his God in every aspect of his life,
As husband, father, teacher, Bible student, friend.

As a husband he would always give encouragement to Mom,
And lead her by the hand most every way.
Their marriage was so solid and let me tell you why,
They'd seek the Lord together every day.

As a father he would discipline whenever we did wrong,
And give us praise whenever we deserved it.
He taught us from God's Word and led us by example,
'Cause he lived his life for God and we observed it.

As a teacher he has left his mark right through the
State of Queensland,
He tried his best to better education.
He influenced as headmaster, a colleague, and a Christian,
And earned the staff and students' admiration.

As a student of the Bible the truth was all he needed,
His passion for God's Word was no illusion.
He believed it as he read it, and he read it as it's written,
So he'd never leave a gap for evolution.

As a friend he was a person you could go to for advice,
Or sit around the table for a chat.
He'd love to take you camping or fishing in his boat,
Now who could want a better mate than that?

So it's with some joy we say goodbye for we know that he is home,
He's with the One that he so much adored.
Yes, he's moved on to a better place and sure we've said goodnight,
But he has said good morning to the Lord.

Thank you, Lord, for Dad.

Stephen Ham

When Steve recited this poem for Dad's memorial service, he also had printed copies to hand to family and friends. I didn't realize however, that one of the verses recited was actually missing in print. The second to the last verse (and I wish to close on this verse) communicates how God's grace affected each of us through my father's life:

So that's our Dad, but more than that, our mentor
    and our friend
And we regret the times we ever gave him strife
But through it all he lost no love but gained some extra zeal
To show us how to live a godly life.

From the beginning of his legacy on Thursday Island in 1928 to the revelation of his legacy at this memorial service in 1995, God used this simple and devoted man to reach a family . . . and then reach the world for the truth and for the Creator. May any and all glory and honor go to the Lord my father served. May any and all thanks go not to my father, but to his Father . . . for that is the way that both of them would want it.

Praise the LORD!
Praise the LORD from the heavens. . . .
Praise Him, sun and moon;
Praise Him all stars of light. . . .

Let them praise the name of the Lord,
For He commanded and they were created. . . .
Beasts and all cattle;
Creeping things and winged fowl:
Kings of the earth and all peoples;
Princes and all judges of the earth;
Both young men and virgins;
Old men and children.
Let them praise the name of the Lord,
For His name alone is exalted;
His glory is above the earth and heaven.

(Ps. 148:1–13)

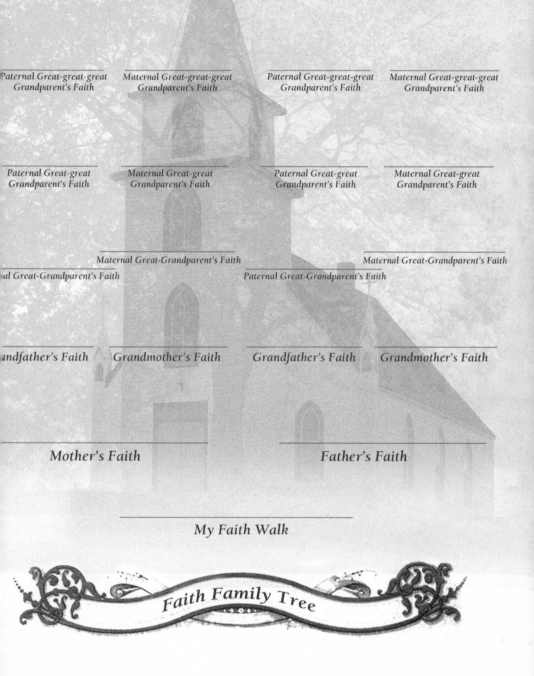

Paternal Great-great-great Grandparent's Faith

Maternal Great-great-great Grandparent's Faith

Paternal Great-great-great Grandparent's Faith

Maternal Great-great-great Grandparent's Faith

Paternal Great-great Grandparent's Faith

Maternal Great-great Grandparent's Faith

Paternal Great-great Grandparent's Faith

Maternal Great-great Grandparent's Faith

Maternal Great-Grandparent's Faith

Maternal Great-Grandparent's Faith

nal Great-Grandparent's Faith

Paternal Great-Grandparent's Faith

andfather's Faith

Grandmother's Faith

Grandfather's Faith

Grandmother's Faith

Mother's Faith

Father's Faith

My Faith Walk

Faith Family Tree

_To:_

From:

My Favorite Scripture is:

Faith Memories

_To:_

From:

Scripture to Celebrate a Joy-filled Day:

Faith Memories

_To:_

From:

Scripture that Gives Me Strength:

Faith Memories

_To:_

From:

I Love this Scripture:

Faith Memories

_To:_

From:

My Favorite Scripture is:

Faith Memories

_To:_

From:

Scripture to Celebrate a Joy-filled Day:

Faith Memories

_To:_

From:

Scripture that Gives Me Strength:

Faith Memories

_To:_

From:

I Love this Scripture:

Faith Memories